'There are many unspoken topics and rules among church culture, and the more work we do to expose those and measure them against the truth of the gospel, the freer the Church will be. This is an important and insightful book that exposes hidden barriers that can prevent people from truly feeling as if they belong – something we all need in order to grow and thrive. It's a challenge to us all to seek to understand and embrace the differences and beautiful diversity that make the Church a place that is welcoming for all.'
Loretta Andrews, music manager, presenter and author

'Here we have two courageous and compelling authors, Natalie and Paul, who have started a really important conversation about a notable divide we find in the UK Church. The class divide. I believe this is prophetically timely, as so many strata of engrained injustice are rightly being societally challenged at present, something Jesus the radical revolutionary epitomized. Anything that prevented the hearts of people having access to him and the good news, he challenged. Within these pages there is a well-articulated, bold and indisputable clarion call to be "seers" of that which needs to be challenged, which is inequitable and is under our nose. Namely a significant body of men, women and children who shouldn't have to do somersaults to enter into the predominantly middle-class Christian culture of the Church. Rather they should be seen, celebrated, empowered and understood, and their cultural assets should be proliferated through every aspect of church life, so that the Church is stronger, representational and diverse. However, the divide first needs to be acknowledged in order to be corporately visible. This excellent book allows us to enter into this acknowledgement. This is a gift to the Church at large.'
Tarn Bright, CEO of Home for Good, author, speaker and advocate

'I'm a Black woman familiar with navigating difficult conversations about inclusivity both in my professional and social circles, so I wasn't expecting to learn anything new about the great cultural divide in UK churches. But here enters humility as I found myself frantically highlighting pages of this book which digs into deep-seated issues with the UK Church. Many church majorities may take offence or say "Why should I?" when it comes to broadening our way of doing things to be more inclusive. But we cannot refuse to change because it doesn't suit us or because it is easier not to. I'm going to be honest here. I think this book on the UK class divide speaks much more to white middle classes than other middle-class or upper-class ethnic groups,

simply because there is a prevailing tendency in Britain generally to treat ethnic minority groups as "other", regardless of economic status. But this is a really helpful and eye-opening handbook for every church, and one which will help ensure that I personally am aligning my ministry – whatever that looks like – to that of Christ and no other.'
Tola Doll Fisher, editor at *Woman Alive*

'*Invisible Divides* is a book for this time. I found myself nodding in agreement at so many points, shocked at some observations and recognizing echoes of how the Church can "other" working-class people, often unwittingly. Natalie and Paul speak powerfully and honestly about the challenges in the Church, and what we can do to correct some of our mistakes.'
Rosie Hopley, founder and former CEO of Beloved

'Inspiringly honest, challengingly thought-provoking and at times painfully relatable, *Invisible Divides* is a refreshing reminder for all who read it that equality is a conscious decision we must choose to make on a daily basis if we hope to eradicate the social divides of classism.'
Claud Jackson, author and trainee vicar

'I'm honoured to call Natalie and Paul good friends and therefore know they live and experience everything they've written in this book. I found reading it very helpful as I'm from another nation and find the whole class system and way of life quite a challenge at times. I don't always know what to do or what's expected of me. Reading this has given me a number of "aha" moments which will help me as I work among different cultures in this nation. I highly recommend it to you.'
Angela Kemm, Senior Leader, City Church Cambridge and Relational Mission

'The marginalizing and "othering" of people who are different is now often seen in relation to issues of race, gender and sexuality. The intense focus on these issues has obscured the issue of how *class* continues to separate and alienate people from one another. *Invisible Divides* shines a light into the culture gap that alienates many working-class people from their local church. Using personal experiences, Paul Brown and Natalie Williams show how they negotiated these issues in their journeys to Christian leadership. They remind us that the radical gospel of Jesus is not some spiritualized version of middle-class values. They challenge Christians to be more self-aware of their

assumptions, deepen their understanding and create a Church that authentically reaches and inspires people from working-class backgrounds.'
Jon Kuhrt, Grace and Truth blog and Government Rough Sleeping Advisor

'If I were to cut myself in half, like a stick of rock, to reveal my greatest passions, you'd see the words: discipleship and prayer. Having read *Invisible Divides*, I was reminded again of the prophetic challenge of the Church to recognize the many ways we need to develop community. As we emerge from our current challenges, there is a need for the Church to have an honest conversation in these areas. This book is a must read especially for leaders looking to be stirred to the many challenges of how we serve prophetically in community. New ways need to be found. The words contained in this book prompted me to pray and ask questions about my own field of ministry and I would invite readers to do the same. This book spoke powerfully and simply to many areas and I'll be coming back to this text again and again. This is needed for such a time as this.'
Adam May, UK Director, Neighbourhood Prayer Network

'I have worked with Natalie and Paul for twenty years, witnessing first hand all the ways in which they have learned to cross divides that other people don't even see. I encourage you to read this book and to learn from their enormous store of wisdom. You will be inspired by their infectious passion and equipped by their practical know-how to cross those invisible divides too.'
Phil Moore, author of the Straight to the Heart series of Bible commentaries

'*Invisible Divides* is a much-needed read for all of us, whatever our experiences of the class system. In this accessible and engaging book, Natalie Williams and Paul Brown shine a light on the unspoken assumptions that shape so much of the culture of church life in Britain. Their winsome blend of humour, theological reflection, anecdote and practical wisdom make this prophetic book a "must buy" for anyone who cares about the Church and its mission today.'
Dr Amy Orr-Ewing, author, speaker and theologian

'In *Invisible Divides*, Natalie Williams and Paul Brown have written a powerful book that can transform church life across the UK and beyond. Their writing comes from a place of deep conviction and personal experience and sheds much light on a crucial area of weakness: our inability to reach and serve many neglected communities across the UK.

'But this book isn't just a practical manual of "dos and don'ts"; rather it's a prophetic cry from the heart of the Father that as the Church, we'd be a place of welcome, a place of meeting, a place of community, a place of hope *for everyone*. Perhaps only then will we have the courage to call on the Lord with *one heart* and *one voice*: "Come, Lord Jesus!"

'Please take the time to let the Lord minister to you through this book.'
Fergus Scarfe, UK Regional Director, GOD TV

'This is an urgent, essential read. I found myself by turns exposed and affirmed in its authentic and deeply personal pages. Articulate, practical and inspirational, Natalie and Paul have hit a bull's eye in bringing these invisible divides into view, but they've also served up a magnificent vision of the dream of God's heart: a kingdom and family on earth unlike any other.'
Akhtar Shah, Director of The Foundry and Dreams Lab

'The gap between the rich and the poor and the middle and working classes has been growing for years and, make no mistake, COVID has only served to speed this up. This book is perfectly timed to speak into the very real issues the Church faces today in serving, supporting and attracting people across all walks of life and empowering them to live out their faith in the setting in which they are placed. Not only are the real-life stories extremely relatable, they also paint the picture of what life and church feel like to so many people in the UK who don't fit in with our middle-class representation of church; it also offers extremely thoughtful and insightful commentary and advice on what we can do about it. Coming from a working-class background myself, I was able to identify with much of what is written and this has helped me to unpack some of my own struggles over the years. While I have found a way to "assimilate" into a middle-class world and a middle-class church environment, this book prompted me to ask questions around why and whether, in retrospect, I should have felt the need to do this. Change is needed if we are going to see thriving churches in this country and this starts with our eyes being opened to the truth around us and what the Bible really says about unity – unity is not homogeny. This book provokes thought and action and needs to be read at every church wanting to transform communities and the lives of people around them.'
Paula Stringer, UK CEO, Christians Against Poverty

'In order to bridge any divide you've got to see it. Natalie Williams and Paul Brown make the invisible visible in this important conversation so we can do just that. Bringing to the fore the experiences and challenges of the working class in our faith communities is helpful for churches and individuals who are committed to unity in our wonderfully diverse nation and beyond.'
Monique Thomas, singer-songwriter, speaker and author

'This book is a wonderful gift to the UK church. *Invisible Divides* helpfully articulates the experiences of the working class while humbly challenging the prevailing middle-class culture to which the Church defaults. Natalie and Paul are a megaphone to the voices of those often overlooked and mis-understood. I truly believe that, if we listen and apply what is written here, our churches will more beautifully reflect the church Jesus longs to return for. This book is Proverbs 31.8 in action!'
Sam Ward, Director of Ministry, The Message Trust

Natalie Williams (@natwillnatter) grew up in a working-class family in Hastings, one of the most deprived towns in the country. She worked as a journalist and has co-authored three books about how Christians in the UK can respond to poverty: *The Myth of the Undeserving Poor* (2014), *A Church for the Poor* (2017) and *A Call to Act* (2020).

Natalie is currently Chief Executive of the UK Christian charity Jubilee+ and Community Engagement Director at King's Church Hastings and Bexhill, where she oversees social action. Natalie is passionate about the mercy of God and Christians actively being mercy-bringers in their communities, especially to those trapped in poverty or injustice.

Paul Brown lives in Bermondsey, south London, with his wife Denise. They have five adult children and, at the last count, 14 grandchildren. He is a church leader and a trade union member and has also served as a school governor and as secretary of his local boxing club. Paul has been a minister at City Hope Church since 1994, having previously worked in the building industry. His passion is to connect with his community and make Jesus known to all, whatever their background. Paul enjoys a good party and watching boxing or football; he has also been known to frequent his local hostelries for a pint with his mates!

INVISIBLE DIVIDES

Class, culture and barriers to
belonging in the Church

Natalie Williams and Paul Brown

First published in Great Britain in 2022

Society for Promoting Christian Knowledge
36 Causton Street
London SW1P 4ST
www.spck.org.uk

British Library Cataloguing-in-Publication Data
A catalogue record for this book is available from the British Library

ISBN 978–0–281–08520–0
eBook ISBN 978–0–281–08521–7

1 3 5 7 9 10 8 6 4 2

eBook by Falcon Oast Graphic Art Ltd

Contents

Contents

Acknowledgements

A book such as this only comes together with the precious insights, stories, life experiences and wisdom of so many people, shared over many years through deep conversations, sometimes funny, sometimes painful, so often inspiring and enriching.

We would like to thank all the people who have shared their stories with us – those who joined us on Zoom in 2020 when the coronavirus pandemic meant we couldn't meet face to face, as well as our friends and those in our church families.

Special thanks to Andy and Ann McWilliam, Ginny Burgin, Tom and Rach Head, Richard Wilson and Martin Charlesworth for reading the first draft and offering such valuable feedback, and to friends such as Angela and Greg Kemm who have encouraged both of us to write on this subject. We would also like to thank Elizabeth Neep and the team at SPCK for their commitment to this book and support through the publishing process.

Natalie would like to thank the teams at Jubilee+ and King's Church Hastings and Bexhill for their ongoing support and encouragement, and her church family who love her well.

Natalie is grateful to the incredible friends who spur on her faith and have supported her during this latest writing endeavour: Hannah Beaney, Andrew Bunt, Louise Cousins, Michelle Earwaker, Santino and Emma Hamberis, Anna Heasman, Claire Lockwood, Pete and Sue Lyndon, Paul and Chloe Mann, Brian Marriott, Paul Mogford, Joanna and Caner Mutu, Liz Nevey, Sarah Owen, Liz Pursglove, Kelly Ramshaw, Jeremy and Ann Simpkins, Faye Thomson, Jon and Al Wales, Richard and Anna Wilson; and her family: Paula and Jonathan, and extra special thanks to her legendary mum Elaine, especially for permission to include some stories about her in this book!

Finally, Natalie would like to thank Denise Brown for faith-building encouragement and lovely lunches, and Paul Brown – thank you for your patience throughout the process; it has been a pleasure to write and share stories with you.

Paul would like to express heartfelt thanks to two special couples, Al and Jane Gregory and John and Mollie Oldfield. They welcomed me and loved me from the moment I first walked into the church. They took a foolish young man who had no knowledge of Jesus and between them they equipped and inspired me to love God, love the church and love the lost. Their example, input, love and patience has had an eternal impact on me.

I must also acknowledge a very special community of people: City Hope Church, Bermondsey. Their passion and humour, their willingness to love, honour and dignify people whatever their class, ability or background, is breathtaking. Thank you for taking such a risk with me when you took me on to the leadership team back in 1994, and thank you for your ongoing prayers and encouragement, especially during the process of writing for this book.

Huge thanks also go to Natalie Williams for trusting me to co-author this book with her! It's been an honour.

Lastly, I could not have written anything without the love and consistent support of a very special woman, Denise Brown, my beautiful wife. A working-class girl from south London, made in the image of God. Your obedience to and love for Jesus is awe inspiring. I love you.

Part 1
IS CLASS AN ISSUE?

Introduction

Natalie's story

I started going to church as a teenager because I liked a boy. I had no real interest in Christianity. I certainly did not intend to become a Christian. Yet six months after my first visit to an evangelical church in Hastings, my home town, I had long forgotten about the boy and had committed my life to Jesus.

Unplanned and unexpected, it was the first surprise of many. Over the following years, I experienced a significant culture shock. I became immersed in a world full of unfamiliarity. The gap between my zealous, angst-ridden atheism and my fledgling faith was huge. So much was new to me. But the chasm between my upbringing and the middle-class behaviour now all around me seemed to be equally vast. It wasn't just that I had so much to learn about Jesus, prayer, the Bible, worship, mercy, justice and all the other essentials of the Christian faith. I felt that I also had to learn all sorts of unknown rules about speech, education, money, meal tables, authority and generally 'right' ways to conduct myself.

Everyday life was suddenly full of new experiences. I felt as out of my depth hanging out with Christians in their homes as I did talking about the doctrine of the Trinity. In fact, it wasn't until I became a Christian that I realized I'd grown up in a working-class family and spent most of my childhood living in relative poverty. I had never really thought about class. I had noticed some things, of course. I knew that some people went to other countries on holiday and had cars that didn't break down often, and had pressure put on them to do well at school. But when I became part of a church – actively involved throughout the week as well as attending on Sunday mornings – I felt out of my depth and out of place. I didn't seem to fit in. I felt different from the majority of the people around me.

Over the years, I have become more middle class in outward appearance. I was pretty good at mimicking the behaviour around me. I picked up some of the rules quickly. Some took longer, but I got there in the end. Friends helped – I remember one telling me that people had noticed that I never brought a food or drink contribution to dinners or parties. It was an unspoken rule that I didn't know about until someone pointed it out to me. Now I bring a bottle usually – though occasionally I deliberately don't, just to see what happens!

Becoming a Christian not only affected my spiritual life, but my aspirations also changed quite quickly. Instead of seeing my life panning out in a specific way and not questioning it, all of a sudden I saw that there might be alternatives. I might have choices.

I was the first person in my extended family to go to university. I struggled my way through with no money and hardly any life skills, but I got a degree and went on to study postgraduate journalism.

Having never travelled overseas with my parents, and having only been on a plane for the first time a week before my twenty-third birthday, I ended up living in China for a year and working as a journalist in Beijing.

More recently, having moved back in with my mum for more than a decade to save up, I became a homeowner. I bought a cheap flat in a deprived part of town – well, cheap by most standards, though it was the absolute most I could get a mortgage for and completely cleared me out. Nevertheless, I now have assets.

During the process of writing this book, several friends told me that I am not working class. It was an interesting experience to have others tell me, sometimes very assertively, what I am and what I am not. I found myself getting very defensive. One friend recently told me that his mix of working- and middle-class experiences means he can easily interact with people from both groups. To be honest, it has not felt like that for me – when people around me tell me their assessment of my class, I am usually left feeling that I have not become middle class enough for the middle classes, but am no longer working class enough for the working classes.

Despite the external trappings of middle classism, I still identify very much as working class. This is a very common experience – many people who identify as working class may not look like it to outsiders. It is hard to define exactly what working class is these days, because it has more to do with internal values than some of the external factors people used to look at, such as what you own, where you work and access to capital. I may have some of the outward signs of being middle class, but I still feel, sound and look working class. I still often feel that I don't fit in, even though I'm part of a lovely church that feels like family. Some of my values and attitudes seem so at odds, still, with those around me.

Does class really matter?

Many people have asked me, over the last few years as I have started to speak and write more openly about my background and experience of church, if class is really still an issue. While writing this book, I have been told countless times that I shouldn't be making a big deal about class issues, because they don't really exist any more. Every single time I have been asked or told that this doesn't matter, it is by someone who is middle class. If anything, the different ways people have responded to the idea of this book show that it is still very much an issue.

It is truthfully the case that no one from a working-class background has asked me if class still matters. In fact, every working-class Christian Paul and I have told about this book has immediately and enthusiastically responded that it is so needed. For the working classes, this is a live and real issue in Britain today, including in our churches. Both of us find that when we speak in churches or even post on social media about this subject, we are frequently approached by working-class people who thank us for highlighting the differences and acknowledging that this is an issue in church life. It often seems that they feel that someone mentioning it from a public platform gives them permission to be themselves.

During the writing of this book, dozens of people have asked us if we want to hear their stories of being misunderstood in churches so that we can include them. For example, a plasterer from London who describes himself as the 'one blue-collar worker' in his church, says he feels 'so out of place most of the time within the church'. He wrote to me, saying:

> It's awesome that you're writing a book on this subject . . . Whenever I've brought this up with people in my church, I've been laughed at or ignored. It's not their fault. They just don't know. I thought I was going mad – that it was just me who felt very different from the rest of the people in my church.

That is one of the reasons we need to talk about class: for the majority in our churches, it isn't on their radar at all, whereas for others it is a very pressing concern in church life. In fact, the differences between us can be a source of great pain for people from working-class backgrounds. It's often why they leave churches.

The under-representation of working-class people in our churches is important because the majority of people in our nation consider themselves to be working class. According to the British Social Attitudes Survey, 60 per cent of people in Britain identify as working class, and, significantly, this proportion has not changed since 1983.[1] It is also worth noting that those who identify as working class are more likely than any others to think that there is 'a wide divide between social classes' – in fact, a massive 82 per cent consider this to be the case.[2]

Those like me, whom society might call 'occupationally middle class' but who identify themselves as working class, are likely to hold similar views to those in traditionally working-class occupations when it comes to social issues.[3] Outwardly, I might look middle class, but inwardly I am still very much working class. The conclusion of the study is this:

> Working class identity remains widespread in Britain. Even though only a minority of people are engaged in working class occupations, a majority of us still think of ourselves as working class . . . social class still has resonance for people.[4]

If research findings are not persuasive enough, when the coronavirus pandemic hit the UK in 2020, it shone a spotlight on deeply entrenched class divisions in our nation. People living in more-deprived areas were twice as likely to die from Covid-19 as those living in more affluent areas.[5] Class is not just a state of mind. It also has serious implications for well-being.

Why does this matter? Specifically, why should it matter to Christians and churches in the UK today?

Since the global financial crash of 2008, many of our churches have really stepped up in terms of social action projects that reach out to people facing poverty or injustice. In some churches, we have seen some of the people who come to our projects also come to faith in Jesus. But often we then struggle to help them find true belonging and community in the church. Specific people come to mind who have encountered Jesus, started to read the Bible excitedly and got baptized with joy, but soon found that their ways of thinking don't quite fit with those around them, and the gap between them and their new friends is just too large – not spiritually, but in every other way. It can feel so overwhelming that it seems insurmountable, so they often leave, feeling that Christianity isn't for them, when in reality it might have simply been that middle-class church wasn't a good fit. It is common to see people from poorer backgrounds – people like me – saved and baptized, but not 'added' (see Acts 2.47).

When it comes to the working class, we are mostly absent from churches: Evangelical Alliance research found that 81 per cent of people in British evangelical churches have a university degree, compared with 27 per cent of the population as a whole.[6]

Churches are not reaching huge sections of our communities. And they are starting to notice.

Churches of all denominations, all across the country, have started to ask the national Christian charity Jubilee+[7] that I work for: how do we help people from working-class backgrounds (including those who are also trapped in poverty) to find family, community and belonging in our churches so that they stick with us and with their new-found faith?

I 'stuck' because of the grace of God, obviously, but I wonder if it was also because I was able to adjust and imitate the behaviour around me. Looking back, I now see that I spent the first 20 years of my Christian life learning how to become middle class because I thought that's what a Christian looks like. Now I am having to disentangle class from the gospel and unlearn some of what I imitated, because though there are many great things about being middle class, there are also some things I never should have picked up.

Over recent years, my heavenly Father has frequently reminded me that the Christian life is about conforming to the image of his Son, Jesus Christ, not conforming to fit in with those around me. In fact, the church is supposed to be a gloriously diverse mix of people from all backgrounds, worshipping side by side with such depth of community that the world around us is astonished by it and drawn to God.

Paul's story

Like Natalie, I remember the culture shock I experienced when I first walked into a church as a 25-year-old bricklayer. I'd only gone because my girlfriend persuaded me. I felt completely out of my comfort zone. I didn't know what to do. I didn't know where to sit or when to stand. The bloke playing the piano and singing was the type me and my mates would have laughed at if he'd walked into our pub.

I knew nothing of God, Jesus or church at all. If I wasn't at work, I was at home with my girlfriend and baby in our little council house or I was going out with my friends – going to football, having a laugh.

Apart from a couple of exceptions, that church was achingly middle class. The people didn't dress like me, they didn't talk like me, they didn't socialize like me. The jobs they did and how they spent their money was so different from me. Even the humour they used was different; nothing was the same.

Years later, while exploring issues of diversity and culture in the church, it became glaringly obvious that the biggest differences were not so much about nationality but much more to do with class issues.

Sadly, the issue of class differences in the church is not a new one.

Anglican minister Roger Lloyd spoke out way back in the 1950s, saying that the working class (or what he called the 'artisan class'):

> constitutes by far the toughest identifiable core of resistance to the gospel today. Up to the present no dents at all have been made in its surface . . . until some more effective way of appealing to the artisan has been found there will be no real revival of religion in this country . . . No amount of success elsewhere will compensate the Church for failure here.[8]

The same theme was being repeated in the 1970s by Dr Martyn Lloyd-Jones:

> The impression has gained currency that to be a Christian, and more especially an evangelical, means that we are

traditionalists . . . I believe that this largely accounts for our failure in this country to make contact with the so-called working classes. Christianity in this country has become a middle-class movement.[9]

And today, the gulf between the Evangelical Church and the working classes in this country is as huge as ever. Presumably that's why in 2012, Tim Chester wrote that 'we are left with a situation in which working-class and deprived areas in the UK are not being reached with the gospel'.[10]

Church for all

In Matthew 5, we read of Jesus saying:

> You are the light of the world – like a city on a hilltop that cannot be hidden. No one lights a lamp and then puts it under a basket. Instead, a lamp is placed on a stand, where it gives light to everyone in the house. In the same way, let your good deeds shine out for all to see, so that everyone will praise your heavenly Father.
> (Matt. 5.14–16 NLT)

Clearly, he expects us to shine for him so that ALL can see. If we want the people of the UK to encounter Jesus, then we need a church that is visible to all, like a city high on the hill. We need a people who are committed to letting the glorious light of Jesus shine out for *everyone* to see!

No one lights a lamp and then covers it up! How absurd would that be? The truth is, when it comes to establishing churches among working-class communities, it seems that it is all too easy to reach for that basket and cover up the gospel light, or maybe shine the light in a different direction. Why is that? Is it because of fear? Fear of people who are different from me and my circle of friends – people whose values, bank balances and life experiences don't match my own?

Social anthropologist Gillian Evans, who came from a comfortable middle-class background but spent more than a decade living on an inner London council estate, highlights not fear but disdain:

> The relationship between the social classes in England hinges on a segregation that is emotionally structured through mutual disdain; in other words . . . the differences between people of distinct classes are deeply felt and not just occupationally defined.
>
> Overcoming them is not, therefore, going to be a simple intellectual decision or even the inevitable outcome of the change in economic fortunes or political will. It is going to be a question of how far we can overcome the embodied and largely unconscious history of how we've come to value ourselves as a particular kind of . . . person.[11]

Sadly, I've experienced evidence of this disdain in the church. I've listened as working-class people have been casually ridiculed and written off by Christians, in a way those same Christians would not dream of treating any other subculture or people group.

I've sat round dinner tables with confident Christian leaders and their families as they've openly and comfortably made value judgements about a person simply because of the size of their television screen and the cost of their Sky TV package, or have talked about not liking certain parts of town and not going there, 'because of the chavs'!

My sincere hope is that those Christian households don't define 'chavs' in the same way as *The Little Book of Chavs*. That particular publication shockingly states that 'chavs' are a 'peasant underclass', and if they're not claiming benefits and hanging around shopping centres and street corners, they have jobs like trainee hairdressers, cleaners, bar staff and security guards. Their diet, according to the book, consists of Pot Noodles, cheap cider and McDonald's for Sunday lunch.[12]

Rather than reinforcing this divisive and negative 'them and us' view, we must make every effort to understand and value the diversity of life experience in the UK and not assume that any way is the best way. The danger in any church where there is a majority culture is that we assume that that culture's habits and traditions and ways of doing things are 'right' and others are 'wrong'. So if most of our churches are predominantly middle class, the chances are that we will very easily slip into believing (subconsciously, at least) that middle-class values are synonymous with Christian values.

The problem is that the existing structures are heavily biased towards middle-class values.

Some of you reading this may feel offended at this point. That is not the intention of this book. We're not trying to make the middle classes feel bad, nor are we saying that working class is better! Rather, what is intended is for us all to understand that the dominant culture in so many churches in the UK is middle class and that middle-class values have become confused with biblical values. We'd like to challenge that. We all need to learn to appreciate the richness and diversity of life expressed by each class. And learn to reject the notions that say, 'My way is the best or only way.'

If this isn't an issue that you have personally encountered, you may be asking if we are making things worse by highlighting differences between the classes. You might think we are making too big a deal of class, and that we would be better off ignoring the subject for the sake of harmony. However, Jesus didn't pray for us to have harmony. He prayed for his followers to have unity:

> I pray also for those who will believe in me through their message, that all of them may be one, Father, just as you are in me and I am in you. May they also be in us so that the world

may believe that you have sent me. I have given them the glory that you gave me, that they may be one as we are one – I in them and you in me – so that they may be brought to complete unity. Then the world will know that you sent me and have loved them even as you have loved me.
(John 17.20–23)

Note that Jesus is saying it is our unity that shows the world that he is sent by the Father and loves his people, and it is this that causes others to believe in him.

We need to completely change our mindset so that we can allow ALL people to enrich us as individuals and as churches. There are some people for whom life is simply a struggle from day one. Countless surveys into child poverty in the UK show that the less you have as you grow up, the more likely you are to face difficulties when it comes to health, education, employment opportunities and even life expectancy. Of course, people from all walks of life suffer. We all have hardships to overcome. But for some, the odds are stacked against them from the moment they are born.

Therefore, if so many of our churches are dominated by the middle classes, the majority may not have experienced the same life issues as the minorities sitting alongside them on Sundays. This is actually why we need one other – to enhance and educate each other about how tough life can be for those who are not like us. We have to engage with people who are different from the majority of our church members. We need to learn their 'language' and culture, find out about their closely held values, discover and understand what they hold dear, and value them for who they are.

I've found that, so often, churches don't seriously consider the working-class communities on their doorstep unless it is in connection with social action. We're willing to run a debt advice centre or a food bank *for* them. There is nothing wrong with these ministries – they are essential – but we must check our attitude and motivation and ask ourselves: are we willing to be on mission *with* people from different backgrounds? Maybe we should also ask ourselves: would I be as confident in my church leader if his background was as a factory worker or a bricklayer, not a banker or a school teacher?

Before I became a Christian, virtually all my friends and family were working class. Almost all the people in my friendship circle were in the building trade in one way or another. It was only after I became a Christian that I slowly learnt to socialize with a new class of people. I can confidently say that I would never have mixed with so many middle-class people. I had to change my attitude, but I can now count doctors and accountants as close friends. That's because we have Jesus in common.

We need to think seriously about the subject of class and the church. We need to completely review our attitudes, our structures and styles, our practice and purpose to ensure we are effectively reaching and including people from working-class communities.

Invisible divides

It might surprise you to know from the start that this book is not really about divisions. It is ultimately about unity in diversity. It is about the church being all it is designed to be: a demonstration of the manifold wisdom of God, where people from all tribes, nations and backgrounds are part of the same body, the same family, the 'one new humanity' in Christ (Eph. 2.15). Jesus demolishes divisions but cultivates diversity.

However, in order to embrace, affirm and value our differences, we need to understand what keeps us apart from those around us. We need to explore the ways in which we might inadvertently exclude, alienate and even offend those who share our faith but not our life experience. We need to see the invisible divides.

Our hope is that by exploring difference, we might bridge some of the invisible divides that would naturally separate us from each other. There are a number of divisions we could touch upon that are extremely important, such as race and ethnicity, or gender, or disability, or even how these intersect, but we are intentionally sticking solely to the issue of class. Even within that, there will be different ways in which class is both experienced and expressed, but we are taking a general overview of class in Britain today. By exploring the issue of class in society and in the church – by acknowledging that there's a missing class – we hope to play our small part in seeing local churches all across the country be more representative of their communities. Just as many churches have a strategy for reaching young people, families or university students, our hope is that majority-middle-class churches might begin to develop strategies to reach the working-class communities around them.

We have picked a handful of areas where we perceive there to be significant differences between classes. These include our approach to faith, how we speak to and about each other, what hospitality looks like, how generosity is expressed, what community means, how we feel about authority, what motivates us, the aspirations we hold for our lives, and our attitudes to and experiences of life and church.

The purpose of this book isn't just to highlight our differences and increase awareness (as valid as that would be), but it's also to help us understand how other people tick, what their experiences are, and to learn from each other and be able to overcome obstacles that might otherwise keep us apart. By highlighting differences, our aim is to create an understanding of the invisible divides so that we might be empowered to cross them. In doing so, we hope that we can discover a depth of unity that we have previously not known. It will require humility on all sides.

The final section of this book is shorter but crucial. We want to provoke discussion about what we can do practically with what we have outlined in this book. How might we change our Sunday meetings to be more inclusive of those who are from a working-class background or join us while trapped in poverty? What might midweek church life look like? Would social gatherings look any different? What about worship, teaching, youth, children's groups, even the notices?

And just as vital: how do we bring people into leadership and influence who look very different from the majority in our churches? Many will agree that it matters that we do this but will not be sure how to go about it. It can prove difficult, but if we want truly diverse churches where people from all walks of life can live in real community with each other, then we must do the hard work of elevating those who may not fit a specific mould of leadership. This is so important and must not be missed. We will never have truly representative churches if we don't bring different types of people into leadership roles.

The disciples would not have chosen each other as Jesus' closest 12. Jewish fishermen would not have wanted to walk closely with a tax collector who made his living by taking from them to give to their oppressors, the Romans. But Jesus brings together people who would not mix by choice. He not only spent a lot of his time with those who were despised, but he also brought together people who would have despised each other. He calls us to a unity and a fellowship that transcend any societal barriers. He calls us to cross invisible divides.

1

The missing class

When I (Paul) first walked into a church meeting, it was difficult to find people like me. People with similar values and interests, a similar accent and job. I quickly realized that this church was very middle class: middle-class attitudes, middle-class values and middle-class social circles all dominated.

I have learnt over the years that my initial experience of church is far from unique. In fact, the dominant culture of the church in the UK typically reflects a middle-class life.

Why are the working classes missing from our churches? There's no simple answer to that question, but throughout this book we seek to highlight some of the complex factors contributing to it. There are a number of reasons why a large section of society is missing from so many of our congregations. We hope to make them visible.

Before we get into some of the specific differences between the classes, let's look at the church.

Leadership

'A church reflects its leaders' is a common phrase and, in general, a true one. To a large extent, a church will mirror the character, personality and style of its leader. If the leader is gregarious and outgoing, typically that will be true of the church. If the leader is a quiet introvert, that will probably be reflected in the people. If the leaders have middle-class values, then we shouldn't be surprised if the congregation is made up of people who share those same cultural values. Craig Groeschel, who leads the multi-campus Life.Church in the USA and created the YouVersion Bible app, which is used by millions of people around the world, runs a popular leadership podcast in which he explains how leaders set the culture of their organizations. This includes businesses, charities and churches. He says, 'Healthy cultures never happen by accident. Your culture [as the leader] is a combination of what you create and what you allow.'[1]

In my experience, church leadership teams are unhealthily dominated by middle-class leaders with middle-class values, and so it can often follow that their congregations are also unhealthily dominated by the middle class. Unhealthy because the church is not supposed to be full of Christian clones – of any shape. Unhealthy because God has called us to be a diverse group of people who only together can demonstrate his manifold wisdom. Unhealthy because we are not effectively reaching out to working-class communities, which means large sections of the population are massively under-represented in our churches.

If we want the working classes in our churches, they need to be represented on our leadership teams. To do that, we need to address deep-seated levels of class bias that honour formal qualifications above all other attributes and reconsider how we develop and train our leaders.

Are we ready to identify and encourage leaders from working-class communities? Are we prepared to take risks with potential leaders whose styles may run counter to the accepted way the church does things? Will we be humble enough to allow our structures and interests to be shaped by working-class values? We explore this in detail in the final section of the book.

God is clearly not just calling the middle classes to leadership. The Revd Lynne Cullens wrote in the *Church Times*:

At a regional church-leadership meeting a few years ago, one of the clergy recounted a phone call that she had received. A young woman with a strong working-class accent had phoned her to ask whether she could discuss a strong call she was feeling to ordination.

When the woman arrived, she was wearing leopard-print leggings and UGG boots, and had bleached blonde hair and eyelashes thick with mascara. The priest expressed amazement at the way in which the woman articulated a passionate personal faith, and a sincere and informed vocation to ministry.

'So, did you put her through to the diocese, then?' she was asked. 'Oh, no!' she laughed. 'Of course not. What would they have made of me sending someone like her through to them?'[2]

'Leggings and UGG boots . . . bleached blonde hair and eyelashes thick with mascara.' Even that description, with its negative undertones, disturbs me. Does it trouble you? Should dress sense, hair colour and being generous with eye make-up exclude a person from a leadership role? Well, it seems in this case, yes! But obviously our answer is a resounding no.

If we want to reach working-class areas in this nation, it matters massively who the church leaders are in those communities. We need to identify leaders from similar backgrounds to those we want to see transformed by the power of the gospel. To do that, we believe we need to change our attitudes and change our structures.

Why is it such a challenge to raise up working-class church leaders? Is it because middle-class culture has been the dominant and default position for too many churches for too long?

Leadership matters – we know that. We know that the personality of the leader shapes the church identity. So why don't we raise up working-class leaders to reach working-class communities? Let's be prepared to change our expectations and existing structures. Let's look for potential leaders who can confidently reach out to working-class communities.

I come from an unmistakeably working-class background. My dad drove a tipper lorry for most of his working life. I'm the oldest of five; none of us went to university, nor did we aspire to. I left school at 16, eventually to get a trade as a bricklayer.

The received wisdom in my family was to get a recognized trade and you would always be in work. And anyway, education past the legal school leaving age wasn't what I wanted – I wanted to get out and earn my own money as soon as possible.

When you learn a building trade, you work alongside an experienced tradesman. You watch, listen and learn. Eventually he will allow you to have a go and you will invariably get it wrong. 'Take it down and build it again.' Eventually you learn by your mistakes. Alongside the learning of skills, you learn the culture of building sites, what is acceptable and what isn't and something about respect for those in authority. Teenage apprentices on building sites are at the bottom of the pile, and they know it!

Sadly, it seems that I'm a rare breed when it comes to church leadership. I've found that, instead of recognizing the value of people from working-class backgrounds and working to develop their leadership skills, much like a skilled brickie and his apprentice, we dismiss them as not having the right skill set or qualifications. Jesus gathered a group of men and women to travel with him from place to place, learning from his teaching and observing how he interacted with people. They had 'on-the-job training' when it came to healing the sick, casting out demons, visiting people's homes and loving the marginalized. They were invited to walk closely with him, discussing what was going on, debriefing as they went, and even being told off by him when they got it wrong or had a bad attitude. By calling people to follow him, Jesus was inviting them not to have teaching from him at arm's length, but to literally follow in his footsteps as apprentices to all he was doing.

If our mission is to be truly relevant and effective, then we need to imitate the example Jesus has set for us, in terms of how we train leaders and who we train. We need to intentionally appoint leaders from backgrounds that are not generally represented on our leadership teams, and in order to do this, we must adopt different ways of developing them so that they can lead effectively.

Church planting

The Bishop of Burnley, Philip North, speaking at the New Wine conference in 2017, said:

> In the inner urban areas and outer estates of our nation there are countless people . . . whose lives are in a mess, who need the saving news of Jesus Christ but who will never hear it. And why not? Because there is no Christian community to proclaim, or because that community is so weak that it has given up . . . The simple and hard truth is that, in the poorest parts of the country, we are withdrawing the preachers. The harvest is rich, but the labourers have been re-deployed to wealthier areas. We are seeing the slow and steady withdrawal of church life from those communities where the poorest people in our nation live.[3]

In my experience, the outreach and church-planting strategies employed by many churches have served to strengthen the dominant middle-class culture of the church. Resources and personnel have been focused on the nicer towns, or certainly the nicer parts of town. Church growth strategy and vision in recent decades has been to establish new churches in university towns by encouraging mobile middle-class Christians to relocate and then focus on reaching people like themselves and the middle-class students. Bishop Philip North, in his challenging talk at the New Wine 'United' conference in 2017, pointed this out when he talked about the Church of England's church-planting strategy. He said, 'The towns chalked down for plants are very clearly identified. They are student towns with a young and upwardly mobile population.'[4] He says that, for the most part, church planting is concerned with middle-class graduates and, according to the bishop, this is one of the factors why churches are in decline: 'We are complicit in the abandonment of the poor . . . The poorer you are, the less the church values you.'[5]

This isn't just the case in the Anglican church; we see the same strategy at work in 'new churches', where church plants typically hire a meeting place accessible to students and the mobile middle classes, often away from the tight-knit working-class communities. An observation Natalie and I have made is that when working-class communities are situated in the town centre, church buildings can often be on the more affluent outskirts, but when the estates are on the periphery, church buildings can usually be found in the centre. Of course, these are generalizations, but looking at church planting across the UK in the last few decades, they appear to be accurate.

This is why it is important to ask ourselves if we are prepared to relocate to areas that are not leafy suburbs, or 'hip and happening' urban enclaves. There are examples of people doing exactly this – it is the way The Message Trust plants churches through its Eden Project, and, notably, Rachel Gardner, who is president of The Girls' Brigade in England and Wales, has moved with her family to Blackburn to plant a church on an estate.

When I told my dad I was moving to Bermondsey, he was horrified, as he saw it as a backward step (ironically, it's now very popular owing to the bite of gentrification). Likewise, when Natalie told her mum she was trying to buy a flat in the most deprived part of town, her mum said she would probably be murdered! But if we want to cross invisible divides, we need to be willing to live in places others don't want to live, and to build relationships with people who are not like us. This includes those who don't earn the same as us or like the same things as us. It might also mean being prepared to put our children in schools that don't have the best reputation, that don't feature at the top of the school league table for the area, that perhaps even have a negative Ofsted review. These are some of the difficult challenges we may have to face if we really want to reach the working-class communities around us.

Our meetings

I remember sitting in church meetings as a brand-new believer. When the preacher got up, we would sit down in quiet rows and listen to a monologue, while many people would be taking notes. To some, our church meetings are more like a schoolroom. Is there an exam at the end of term? Is this because middle-class people are more comfortable with a formal learning setting? Maybe that's why some churches make their children's work resemble a classroom.

Yet we tell people that church is family.

The problem here is people's widely differing experiences of family gatherings. For some, it's a polite, pre-planned get-together. There might be intellectually interesting conversation while the children play in another room, out of earshot. For others, all ages are crammed into one room. There is simultaneous shouting, electronic games, children running round, loud conversations and even louder music.

One of the reasons that the working classes are missing from our churches is because our meetings are not culturally comfortable for them. We elaborate on this in some detail further on in the book.

Outreach programmes

Our outreach activities can actually exclude the working classes. Our programmes can easily – even if this is mostly unconscious – reinforce a class bias.

Some churches will charge a ticket price for outreach events they are hosting, automatically excluding those living on a tight budget. We might say when announcing these events that if money is an obstacle, people should come to talk to us so we can help, but that places them in the undignified situation of coming cap in hand to ask for help to come to an event that presumably we want them to attend.

Alternatively, the nature of the event itself could be much more likely to appeal to a middle-class audience. A classic example of this was a cheese and wine evening hosted by a church plant I (Paul) was part of. With high expectations, the church hired a hall on a sprawling suburban council estate. The evening was planned as a social event to reach out and get to know the people of that community. As the night progressed, it took an interesting turn when one of the larger-than-life local characters decided he would liberate a bottle or two of the wine and, instead of sipping Rioja from the dainty glasses provided, proceeded to glug directly from the bottle. He then went on to forcefully and very vocally demand access to the microphone. Thankfully, the host managed to keep a tight grip on that mic! The result of his antics was that the evening wasn't the success people had anticipated!

In contrast, I have positive memories of a karaoke outreach event in my early days in Bermondsey, south London. This was when it was still a proud working-class community, before gentrification had changed the landscape. The church building was packed with a large number of local characters and the event was a roaring success. Loads of locals seemed to be culturally connected and very comfortable in a church building at this kind of event, and they were happy to listen to personal stories of salvation, even though the hymns had been replaced with out-of-tune renditions of 'I'm too sexy for my shirt' and 'Like a virgin'!

The raucous karaoke evening certainly went down much better than the polite wine-tasting event on that council estate. Some outreach events are simply ill-informed for the people who live in the area. Of course, there are some social events that cross class barriers, such as pub quizzes, or even combine different aspects to appeal to different groups. In Natalie's church, a photo exhibition with a hog roast went down well with people from different backgrounds, some drawn by the food while others came for the art, and everyone seemed to enjoy the bar!

There is a lesson to be learnt here: we need to know our target audience(s) and what appeals to different groups of people, as well as what puts them off. Also, as we explore later in the book, we must not despise the different ways people spend their leisure time.

Our resources

Our resources and courses are often focused on and geared to the middle classes. A few years ago, I attended an outreach conference in central London. The underlying theory put forward was for churches to focus their outreach on the 'movers and shakers' in society, those working in media, the influential politicians and wealthy financiers. This is an outreach strategy that has some similarity to trickle-down economics, the theory favoured by some politicians, where tax breaks and other incentives for big business and the wealthy will eventually benefit the rest of society through investment and job creation.

The Revd Gary Jenkins wrote:

> The trickledown theory of mission (focus on the rich, powerful, clever and the influential first in order that the effect may trickle down to the lower orders in due course), much loved by English evangelicals, is not only contrary to the grain of Scripture but has demonstrably failed. Rather, the effect of this policy has been to produce a strongly middle-class church, peculiarly ill-suited to ministry among working class people.[6]

Revival typically starts among working-class communities. Culture-changing gospel advance in the UK has almost always been among the working class. So if these groups are missing from our churches today, we should be deeply concerned about that and working hard to address it.

In the nineteenth century, the Salvation Army was far from being a respectable middle-class movement. Founder William Booth's converts and those who went on to join him in his missionary work were drawn from the poorer end of Victorian society. They came not just to hear the gospel, but also to access food, clothing and even jobs. As a result, the Salvation Army understood working-class people and their values. It was able to communicate comfortably with the people ignored by the middle-class churches of the day. This contributed significantly to the success of the Salvation Army's mission among working-class Victorians. Some of its leading evangelists emerged from the ranks of the working-class communities they were reaching into.

Almost 100 years before the Salvation Army, the Industrial Revolution brought about social change in eighteenth-century Britain. Cities grew rapidly as the rural population moved in great numbers in pursuit of work. Alongside the dramatic increase in urban populations, there was an increase in poverty and social deprivation. By all accounts, the established church at the time was not much more than a cosy club for the affluent middle classes. Most clergymen had no understanding or care for the needs of the working class, probably because they were drawn from the same circles as their well-heeled parishioners.

Methodist pioneers – George Whitefield, the Wesley brothers and others – were led to focus on the neglected sections of society. People from these communities were not always welcome in churches. I (Paul) have visited Anglican churches that still have in place the rooms where poorer people were put so they could hear the preacher, but not see him.

Segregation by class really happened in our churches. That's one of the reasons why Whitefield, the Wesleys and others took the gospel out to the people whom others wouldn't allow in. So they preached outside coal mines and in market squares, on heaths and in fields. The working class were given the attention they were denied by the established church. And, as a result, thousands were saved and added to the kingdom.

The apostle Paul wrote to the church at Corinth:

Not many of you were wise by human standards; not many were influential; not many were of noble birth. But God chose the foolish things of the world to shame the wise, God chose what is weak in the world to shame the strong.
(1 Cor. 1.26–27)

If we want to see the spiritual landscape change again, like it did in the days of William Booth and George Whitefield, there is an urgent need for us to apply these words that the apostle Paul wrote to the Corinthian church.

People or projects?

How we greet people and how we treat people has a huge impact on whether they stick with a church or disappear after a little while. Social action projects have sprung up in churches of all kinds across the nation since the global financial crash in 2008. These have provided vital practical support to people facing crisis situations. Most project leaders and volunteers have a desperate desire to give dignity to everyone they help. However, any one of us can slip into a 'saviour complex' that gives us an air of superiority – this is something we all need to watch in our own hearts. Also, no matter how much we try to run our projects in a way that honours people, there is something inherently undignified about turning up at an unfamiliar location where everyone knows you are in need. Providing support for people facing hard times is essential, but we need to recognize that there is an automatic power imbalance whenever we do this that some people can find very difficult to overcome.

Of course, acts of generosity and support are necessary and important, but there are times when they can cause resentment in the very people they are set up to support. People can feel patronized and belittled by acts of charity if they perceive an attitude of superiority among those who are supporting them. For example, a couple of years ago, a neighbour of mine (Paul) had lost his job and was struggling as a single parent with five kids. I remember him getting very angry when a neighbour turned up at his door to present him with a food parcel. Undoubtedly, she was trying to be kind, but as far as he was concerned, he wasn't a charity case, and he resented the fact that his neighbour thought he was!

The Revd Jenkins puts it quite starkly when he says, 'Middle class Christians enjoy helping the poor much more than the poor enjoy being helped.'[7] That isn't always the case, but we do need to be wise when we offer that kind of support and work very hard at maintaining people's dignity at all times. This can be one of the reasons it's so hard to cross invisible divides: while some may be overwhelmed with gratitude for our support, others may feel offended by it. That is why we need to have open dialogue between those helping and those being helped, and to be willing to hear how our support is received.

Attitudes and values

Another reason the working class are missing from our churches is the vast difference in our attitudes and values. We expand on this in Part 2. Many of us have an ingrained instinct when it comes to what is valued in life, what is acceptable and what is not.

I've encountered the 'shock, horror' attitude some Christians have shown to cigarette smokers – complaining about people smoking outside the church building, for example. But are we really going to make smoking a stumbling block to people feeling welcome among us? Are people missing from our churches because they were made to feel unwelcome simply because they smoke? I've hosted Alpha courses where just putting a couple of smoke breaks into each session makes people feel at ease and welcome. It is an easy thing to do, and it makes a bigger difference to people feeling accepted and welcomed than we might imagine.

I recall the time a mature Christian friend was showing me his expensive, newly installed bathroom (to him, a wise investment) while at the same time deriding people who live in a modest flat and buy a huge flat-screen television (to him, a foolish waste of money). Many of us can fail to notice the irony in our own attitudes. For example, we might think it is perfectly OK to pay a large monthly subscription to the golf club while we frown on someone who buys a weekly lottery ticket; or we might think it is impressive when someone tells us about their subscription to a fine wine society but we might not approve of someone's habit of stopping off at the local pub every night after work.

Whatever background we are from, the gospel challenges us to change our attitudes to people around us who are different. The question for us as Christians is: are we willing to do this? This may require us to let go of long-held values that have their roots in a class structure, not in Scripture. We can underestimate how difficult and costly it is to change, but we need to make those changes if we want to reach the large swathes of society who are currently missing from our churches. For those of you readers who recognize you are in the dominant culture in your church, the toughest thing of all might be agreeing to actions that will broaden your church's appeal to other groups of people and simultaneously push you out of your comfort zone. Part of this includes laying down your power and preferences and empowering others; not just listening to them, but also sometimes letting their voices be louder than yours.

The dominant class and culture in the UK church is middle class. If we really want to address the lack of working-class believers, then the middle-class church needs to make radical changes and do things very differently. 'But don't the working classes also need to make changes?' you might ask. Yes, we all do, but the onus is on the dominant culture to make space for those who are missing among us. That's going to hurt, especially if those in the church have enjoyed some successes reaching out to their middle-class peers and don't see the need to change. Change is usually met with resistance and is often painful. For example, if those changes impact who is on our leadership team or staff team, and how we do mission, or if we decide to change our structures and preaching styles, it will probably be very uncomfortable. But if we don't make changes, church attendance will continue to shrink, and working-class communities will not encounter Jesus. Or if they do, it will be despite the church, not because of us.

It is healthy to ask ourselves if we need to do things differently. It is good to consider why we do the things we do. If we want to change the demographic of our churches, we will need to change those ways of behaving, the unspoken and unwritten rules, the invisible divides that cause people to feel like outsiders unless they conform to the dominant culture.

Do your church structures and traditions alienate those from working-class backgrounds? We hope this book will help you to answer that question. Are you willing to make changes if those changes mean working-class communities will feel accepted and at ease in your church and even in your home? If we are willing to change, then the working classes are much more likely to thrive in our churches.

This is an issue the whole church needs to grapple with, however difficult or painful it might be.

Mike Savage and Fiona Devine's 'Great British Class Survey', with its innovative way of categorizing class, would say that 48 per cent of the working population are drawn from three identifiable main groups: the Traditional Working Class, the Emergent Service Sector and the Precariat.[8] (The 'Precariat' are those whose daily lives are precarious – they are the most deprived.) Whether we are talking about people who self-identify as working class, those who are living on the cusp of poverty, those in traditional working-class jobs or those who live hand to mouth, whichever way you look at it, that's a lot of people not being effectively reached by our churches. That's a lot of people we are missing. It's a lot of people who are loved by God and whom he wants to see in our churches.

2

The call to discipleship

Discipleship is a vital part of the Christian life. Jesus told his disciples to make disciples. It is something that everyone who follows him is called to do. But when it comes to actually helping others to mature in their faith, it is so easy to disciple them into our way of doing things. Christians are called to be conformed to the image of Christ, but so often, if we are not mindful of it, we can try to conform ourselves or others to the traditions and habits of our church community.

This means that if the majority in a particular church is middle class, we can easily fall into the trap of discipling people into our middle-class ways, rather than into becoming increasingly like Jesus. It can be hard to tell the difference between what we are used to and what is Christlike.

For many years, I (Natalie) was told by various Christian friends that I should try to buy my own home – that I should 'get on the property ladder'. Though not stated quite this explicitly, I picked up in my twenties that home ownership is important and something I should aspire to. I don't recall ever being told why, from a biblical point of view. I just took it on board, without understanding it and without asking what made it so important. I do remember a sermon I heard as a teenager where the preacher exclaimed passionately that owning a home was not important because it was 'all going to burn!' and it might stop you from becoming an overseas missionary. But aside from that, everything I was told led me to assume that owning your own home must be a key Christian principle. I cannot remember ever dreaming of owning my own home as a child – I don't think I ever thought about it until friends in the church started talking to me about it.

It is only in more recent years – and ironically since I started to look into buying a flat and then managed to do so – that I have questioned whether this is part of being a 'good Christian' or if it is actually just a middle-class value. Over the years, it has been re-iterated to me time and time again that owning property is better stewardship of my money and the wisest course of action in terms of security for the future. Both of these arguments influenced my understanding to the point where I started to think a decision about property was a reflection of my maturity as a Christian and, without realizing this was happening, I started to conflate home ownership with godly living.

There are lots of benefits to owning your own home, of course. But my point is more that I was, in effect, discipled into it as if I would somehow be more Christlike if I owned property. That's quite ironic seeing as Jesus didn't own his own home!

External values

So much of our discipleship is focused on external values such as this. We encourage new converts to give up smoking, swearing, drinking, gambling and so on, while ignoring more socially ac-ceptable middle-class sins such as coveting, envy, malice, gossip, pride, slander, greed, gluttony and the rest. Gary Jenkins says, 'The church has tended to be sterner on working class sins than middle class ones.'[1]

Jesus said that all of these things – the ones we consider to be 'big' sins and those we don't find so offensive or objectionable – come from our hearts (see Mark 7.20–23). Yet we so rarely challenge each other about pride or gluttony, or even lying, which the Bible says is 'detestable' to God (Prov. 6.16–19). And these can be curiously absent from our discipleship materials too.

This isn't to say we shouldn't be concerned with the external things. We should. But our tendency to focus on them more than on internal things can create barriers for people who are new or imma-ture in their faith. When I returned from a few years of backsliding, many Christians around me were concerned about my smoking. Of course, when I eventually gave up (almost four years after coming back to my faith in Jesus), I knew it was what God wanted for me – that he was concerned with my physical health and how much money I was spending on cigarettes. But God is patient with us. When I initially returned to him, his focus with me seemed to be on dealing with some painful things I was carrying, and knitting me into a church community. That might sound like an excuse to carry on smoking, but nearly 20 years on, I look back and see how God was gently and tenderly dealing with different things in my heart and behaviours at his pace.

While many Christians around me would say every Sunday (when I popped outside to smoke between the singing and the sermon, or afterwards when I would be outside smoking as soon as the service finished), 'God wants you to quit smoking,' or, 'Haven't you given that up yet?' it didn't seem at the time (or looking back now) to be God's priority for me. At the time I was in a small group where there was never any pressure to give up smoking. In fact, usually one or two people would stand outside with me and talk to me while I smoked, and one member of the group even used to let me smoke in her home if I sat by the chimney. This group helped me to change some of the habits that I felt I should kick – things like watching hours of soaps on TV – and some of my attitudes that I knew needed to change, such as to money and work. They even bought me a car when I needed one for work, even though I was still spending my money on cigarettes and other things in-stead of putting it towards a car myself. Their kindness in discipling me was transformative. Through them, God changed many areas of my life.

When I talk with people who were in that group with me back then, most conversations include some reflection on how different

I am now. Sometimes I am reminded of things I had forgotten. Just this week, someone mentioned that I used to wear a baseball cap all the time, so that I could hide behind it – something I can't even imagine doing now.

The point is this: discipleship that was effective for me as an immature Christian, from a different background from many of the people around me, was focused much more on loving me, praying for me, encouraging me and letting the Holy Spirit do his work than on pointing out to me the external things I was doing wrong. Of course, discipleship is fundamentally about obedience to Jesus. The group leaders and various friends in the group did challenge me – it wasn't that they never mentioned things I was doing – but they gave me time, and they focused on the areas God was highlighting and encouraged me in those areas first and foremost. I am very grateful for that small group, because I think without their patience and gentleness, I would not have stayed around in church life for long.

That said, now that I am so acquainted with middle-class church life and have outwardly become quite middle class myself, I have found myself doing exactly the same to people from working-class backgrounds as I am describing! A few years ago, I was trying to support a friend from one of the local estates and I was focusing on how much alcohol she drank and her weekend going-out habits. I talked to her about it a few times, and nothing changed. What was interesting, though, is that when I stopped focusing on that and instead fixed on how we were both loving Jesus well in our day-to-day lives, she came to her own conclusions about drinking so much. One day, unprompted by me, she said, 'Nat, I feel the Holy Spirit telling me I need to drive when I go out at the weekends so that I won't drink so much.' As she told me that, I smiled as I realized that the Holy Spirit is very good at his job.

As I have already written, that's not to say we shouldn't challenge people. Jesus said that we show our love for him by obeying his commands, so we should challenge each other. But when we do, we should consider two things. First of all, is this an issue of becoming like Jesus, or of becoming like the majority in church (for example, home ownership)? Second, am I focusing on the same areas God is currently focusing on with this person, or are some sins more troublesome to me than others (getting drunk compared to envy, for example)?

Two-way discipleship

I am convinced that we would 'keep' more people from a working-class background – and more people who are in poverty, too – in our churches if we took some time to really think through our discipleship culture, and what we might be inadvertently communicating by the things we focus on.

I also believe wholeheartedly that discipleship should be two way, and that even when we are discipling someone we should be expectant for God to teach us just as much as he teaches the person we are discipling. The New Testament talks about 'one anothering' an awful lot.[2] So even when we are the more mature believer, there is plenty we can learn from the person we are helping to grow. I would argue this is especially true when that person's background is different from ours. When I spend time with people who are 'not like me', it broadens my outlook, challenges my ingrained perspectives and exposes me to different ways of seeing things. My life is enriched by walking alongside people who have very different life experiences. So is my faith. It is deepened and strengthened when I hear viewpoints and stories that are unfamiliar to me.

Part of effective discipleship has to include challenging our own preconceived ideas. When I speak at various churches across the UK, I often arrive the previous day or stay after the service and spend time with the leadership team or social activists in the church. Without fail, on these occasions when I answer questions about pouring out our lives for others – especially when it comes to mercy, compassion and generosity – I am asked where we should (and where we are allowed to) draw the line. The question seems to be based on, 'How much can I keep?' or, 'How much do I *have* to do?' rather than wanting to lean into these things as much as possible. Frequently, within this bigger question, there is a smaller, specific one about what we do with our own money: how much should we spend, give and save?

I find this question fascinating because it usually comes with the underlying assumption that saving money is biblical. I have been taught on Christian leadership training courses that saving at least 10 per cent is good stewardship, and Paul has similarly heard Christian leaders encouraging church members to tithe 10 per cent and save 10 per cent of their income. I am not so sure that saving is as biblical as we make out, but that is often not a well-received opinion! Please hear me out. I am not saying that we shouldn't be good stewards – we should absolutely prove ourselves faithful with whatever God has entrusted to us, in all areas of life. But I cannot see any biblical basis for accumulating savings. In fact, there are several Bible verses about not hoarding wealth: in Ecclesiastes it says that riches being hoarded is 'a grievous evil' that can hurt the owner (Eccles. 5.13); Paul writes to Timothy that desiring to be rich can lead to temptation, snare, harm, ruin and destruction, adding that 'the love of money is a root of all kinds of evil' (1 Tim. 6.9–10); Jesus himself said we should not store up treasures for ourselves, and he challenged a rich young man to give away all he had (Matt. 6.19; 19.21); and James warns us against laying up treasure and living 'in luxury and self-indulgence' (Jas. 5.1–5).

In my last book, my co-author Martin Charlesworth, who is himself middle class, posed this challenge to all Christians by reminding us that we are called to simplify our lives. Martin quotes Proverbs 30.8–9, which says, 'Give me neither poverty nor riches, but give me only my daily bread. Otherwise, I may have too much and disown you . . . Or I may become poor and steal, and so dishonour the name of my God', and makes the point that followers of Jesus are to live simple lives, where we give away more than we hoard for ourselves.[3]

This is a hard teaching in a middle-class context, because it goes against what comes naturally and has been instilled as wisdom. This struck me recently because I recognized that I had taken on this middle-class value as if it was the way Christ lived. Clearly it wasn't how he lived, or what he taught. But somehow I had subsumed it into my idea of biblical values. The truth is that if we have plenty of money in the bank, we never have to live by faith. Also, God has been challenging me over the last few years about whether it is ever permissible for me to have way more than I need when there are people around me who don't have the basics they need. I'm certain the answer is a resounding 'no'!

I am not saying we should never save any money – we explore this more in the chapter on generosity later in the book. I am simply using this as an example – and a provocation, hopefully – about some of our ways of thinking that may have more to do with our upbringing, background and experiences than they do with biblical discipleship. My aim isn't to encourage us to never save, but rather to seriously consider whether our values (on a whole range of subjects) are middle class or biblical. They will sometimes be both, but sometimes they won't line up, and then we have to choose which we will follow!

Questioning our assumptions

We are all informed and make decisions based on underlying assumptions. The hope behind this chapter is just that we might begin to question them. Some we will question and stick with, deciding that they are indeed Christlike. Others we will need to change.

Among the discipleship areas we might want to pause to consider are assumptions along the lines of:

- home ownership is better than renting;
- saving money is better than giving it away;
- the longer you stay in education the better;
- you should choose carefully the neighbourhood where you live;
- you should try to send your children to the highest-achieving school;
- being organized with a diary is a sign of spiritual maturity.

These are just a few, based on conversations I have had over the last few years. There will be many more. Our assumptions can particularly reveal themselves when we are looking to entrust people in church with responsibility and/or leadership. We will look at this in more detail later, but an example of a key question I would urge us to ask is this: is calling someone to be faithful with the small things the same as calling someone to be good with a diary?

We are all called to make disciples, but it is so important that we remember we are discipling people to become like Jesus, not like us. How we do this is simple: it has more to do with sharing our lives than with a weekly or fortnightly appointment to check how someone's Bible reading and prayer times are going. It isn't just about getting involved in other people's lives, but also about letting them get involved in yours. Are you willing to learn from the person you're discipling?

The settings we use for discipleship are important too. If we mimic academic settings, or even expect people to come to dinner at someone's home when that's not a familiar thing for them to do, is that the most helpful way to disciple people who are not used to those environments? I often think about how weird it is, for example, to have a group of adults standing around and singing in someone's living room!

It takes time to make disciples. In our quick-fix, instant-fame, microwave society we can so easily see sanctification as something that should happen overnight in those we are discipling, while forgetting that it's an ongoing process of God's work in us. In the end, it took me eight attempts to give up smoking, but God was at work. Learning some life skills that I previously lacked has taken longer. Getting out of debt took several years, but God was at work. We are all works in progress.

Part 2

DIFFERENT WAYS WE THINK AND ACT

3

Faith

I (Natalie) always seem to find myself sitting next to a friend from one of the local estates on any Sunday morning when someone preaches about living by faith. It is not intentional. It just seems to turn out that way. The reason I know this is because the comments afterwards are sometimes quite colourful, and always memorable. The reaction is normally in connection with the examples given or stories told.

For example, during a sermon on faith, a well-known guest speaker shared a faith story from his own life. He explained that he had bought a house, and it had been a significant financial stretch for him, so he couldn't afford to go on holiday that summer. For him, this was a faith battle. He shared that he felt God wanted him to have a holiday, so he prayed for it. He asked God to provide a holiday for him, and he did. Someone unexpectedly offered their home while they were away. Another person anonymously dropped an envelope full of money through his door, which covered travel costs and gave him some spending money.

Now, there is nothing wrong with this. For the person who shared it on that Sunday morning, it was a genuine story of having faith in and praying for God's provision. The vast majority of people in the congregation on that particular Sunday would have been able to relate to it. It would have resonated with them, encouraged them and spurred them on in their faith. It was a good story.

However, for others, like the friend sitting next to me, it spoke of extraordinary privilege. In fact, as soon as the sermon ended, my friend turned to me and said something along the lines of, 'Why would someone be sad that they couldn't go on holiday if they'd just managed to buy their own home?' She could not relate to the story – in fact, she couldn't get her head around it at all.

Please do not misunderstand this point. It is good and right for ministers and preachers to give authentic examples from their own lives. They cannot make up need where it doesn't exist, nor should they edit or sanitize their stories so that no one is offended by or disconnected from what they are saying.

But it is important to recognize that our life experiences are not the same as everyone else's, and it can be especially alienating for those who have less than we do materially if we talk about faith in terms of gaining luxuries, without adding any caveats or examples from other people's lives.

Faith battles

When it comes to provision in particular, the faith battles of someone who lives in a constant state of asking God to provide are very different from the faith battles of someone who has all the essentials. There are many ways in which different groups of people exercise and express faith, but in this chapter we will focus on faith when it comes to provision.

The most incredible stories of faith I hear actually always come from those who are in desperate or significant need. Some of my friends have faith story after faith story of God's provision in their lives – because they have to; because if God doesn't come through for them they literally won't have food or shelter or clothing. Passages of the Bible such as Matthew 6.25–32 take on a much deeper and more precious meaning when you are literally seeking God for food for the week. Jesus said:

Therefore I tell you, do not be anxious about your life, what you will eat or what you will drink, nor about your body, what you will put on. Is not life more than food, and the body more than clothing? Look at the birds of the air: they neither sow nor reap nor gather into barns, and yet your heavenly Father feeds them. Are you not of more value than they? And which of you by being anxious can add a single hour to his span of life? And why are you anxious about clothing? Consider the lilies of the field, how they grow: they neither toil nor spin, yet I tell you, even Solomon in all his glory was not arrayed like one of these. But if God so clothes the grass of the field, which today is alive and tomorrow is thrown into the oven, will he not much more clothe you, O you of little faith? Therefore do not be anxious, saying, 'What shall we eat?' or 'What shall we drink?' or 'What shall we wear?' For the Gentiles seek after all these things, and your heavenly Father knows that you need them all.

(Matt. 6.25–32 ESV UK)

For those of us who live affluent or even relatively comfortable lives, these words of Jesus are nice, but we don't have to exercise meaningful faith to believe them literally. However, for those who live on low incomes, these are words to grab hold of, pray earnestly and remind God of his promises.

This became more obvious (in the UK, at least) during the coronavirus pandemic. In the initial few months, there was a lot of talk in the public sphere about us all being in the same boat, and Covid-19 being the great leveller. The pandemic affected everyone in one way or another. Savings in the bank or a high-earning job could not necessarily protect anyone from the virus. People of all classes got sick and died.

In my last book, *A Call to Act*, I wrote about my own experiences of losing some of my income as a result of the pandemic during the first lockdown in the UK. I also wrote about other ways in which that first lockdown – when we were only allowed out for essential work, shopping and one walk a day, and before 'bubbles' were introduced – affected me, as someone who lives in a flat without a garden, for example.[1] But what really struck me a few weeks into that lockdown was the stark contrast between the faith required (in general) by my working-class friends and the ways in which my middle-class friends were experiencing the pandemic.

It became clear very quickly that for my more comfortable friends (and for me, too), the faith journey through coronavirus had very little to do with financial catastrophe and more to do with inconvenience. This was not true across the board – some of my comfortable friends experienced incalculable grief as they lost loved ones. But in terms of getting through from week to week, it was quickly obvious that we were not 'all in the same boat' after all. While the virus itself was indiscriminate, its impact on people's day-to-day lives was felt most acutely by those either in poverty or on low incomes.

Let me elaborate. Some aspects of the pandemic and associated lockdowns were experienced by people of all classes, on all income levels. Solicitors were furloughed from their jobs as well as coffee shop baristas. When I lost almost 25 per cent of my income overnight, I was able to weather it because I was spending less owing to lockdown, had modest savings in the bank and within a couple of months I was able to increase my hours at a different job. The first lockdown had a noticeable impact upon me, but I was grateful for God's provision, which meant it didn't require huge faith to get through it. I did pray about my situation, but I knew I would be OK so I didn't really need to seek God as earnestly as many others did during that time.

But for some of my friends, it was a very different story. The lowest paid were the most likely to have been furloughed.[2] Cleaners, construction labourers, security guards, hairdressers, retail staff, care workers, administrators, waiters and waitresses – these were among the professions most likely to be furloughed and therefore most at risk of losing one-fifth of their income. For Christians in these professions, their faith instantly became very active and real as the first lockdown took place.

Whereas those earning moderate or high salaries could more easily get through the pandemic by making adjustments to their lifestyle, those earning less were not in a position to make simple changes to do with optional extras or luxuries. For many of those who lost 20 per cent of their income when they were furloughed, that was the percentage they had been spending on food each month. We saw literally hundreds of people at my local food bank in this situation. 'Adjustments', in these cases, meant choices such as eating or falling into rent arrears, or getting into debt so they could pay for reliable broadband so that their children could continue their education at home, even in one case selling all of their downstairs furniture to buy food.

When your choices are feeding your family or risking eviction, the words of Jesus in Matthew 6 take on new meaning, and require a great deal of practical, demonstrable faith.

God's amazing provision

One of my working-class friends has the best stories of God's provision. She frequently needs him to come through for her, and he always does. One of her stories that I love is that she was having an argument with her teenage daughter, who then threw her mobile phone across the room. The screen was smashed, making it unusable. My friend felt that God wanted her to have the phone repaired, as an example of grace to her daughter, but she couldn't really afford to. However, she responded to God's prompting in faith. Taking her last £40, she went to a shop and paid them to repair the phone.

Later, the owner of the repair shop called my friend and said, 'When you gave us the £40, there was a £50 note between the notes you gave us. So when you come back to pick up the phone, we'll return it to you.'

My friend assured them that she hadn't accidentally given them £50! But they were adamant that it must be hers because they hadn't had any other customers pay by cash that day. Despite the fact that she told them it wasn't hers, they insisted she take the £50 note.

I love that when she obeyed God with the gracious act of fixing her daughter's phone, God not only reimbursed my friend her last £40, but also gave her an extra £10 on top! This is a story of what God does when our faith needs him to work wonders on our behalf.

Now, of course, people of all classes and all income levels have experiences in life that require faith. My point is simply that there's a level of urgency to faith – for all of us – when we have no control over our circumstances. That happens to everyone at one time or another. A business collapsing or a terminal diagnosis, a sudden loss or an unforeseen marriage breakdown – there are any number of awful experiences that affect people from all walks of life, leading us to cry out to God in faith when the odds are stacked against us.

My argument is that for those who live from hand to mouth, the need to urgently cry out to God in faith comes around much more often than for those who live in relative comfort. This is not just an observation from looking around at church life. I believe it is clearly revealed in the Bible too. Jesus said, 'Blessed are you who are poor, for yours is the kingdom of God' (Luke 6.20). Jesus seems to be saying here that those who have very little in this life will inherit spiritual things of greater worth than the money, possessions and assets some of us can accumulate.

Rich in faith

James states it plainly too: 'Listen, my beloved brothers, has not God chosen those who are poor in the world to be rich in faith and heirs of the kingdom, which he has promised to those who love him?' (Jas. 2.5 ESV UK). It seems that God grants a rich, vibrant faith to those who have the least in this life. This is most evident in developing nations. I have had the privilege of being taken on work-related trips to Kenya, Cambodia and India in the last few years. In each of these places I have met Christians who have far, far less materially than I have, yet have an incredible, joy-filled faith that made me feel envious of them. I have more money and own more stuff than the vast majority of believers I met in these countries, but their faith is so much richer than mine. God really has granted those who are poor in this world a richness in faith.

This is true in our churches too. The faith of those who have less is often not just richer than the faith of those who are financially rich, but it is usually also real, raw and profoundly inspiring. Yet we can miss it if we are not paying careful attention. There are those among us who are like the widow Jesus points out to his disciples in Luke 21.1–4:

> Jesus looked up and saw the rich putting their gifts into the offering box, and he saw a poor widow put in two small copper coins. And he said, 'Truly, I tell you, this poor widow has put in more than all of them. For they all contributed out of their abundance, but she out of her poverty put in all she had to live on.'

In our churches today, we might go so far as to counsel someone against this. I know I have offered what I thought was 'wise counsel', only to later feel the gentle conviction of the Holy Spirit that I leapt to offer sensible advice rather than encourage someone's step of radical faith. On the flipside, we can so easily fall into the danger of only appreciating gifts that are financially substantial. We discussed this dilemma in my church leadership team during the coronavirus pandemic. Many church members gave *more* generously at that time – either to the church in general or to our food bank and other social action projects. We wanted to express gratitude (rightly so), but it was hard to figure out how to. Should we write 'thank you' cards to those who had given more than a certain amount? Reflecting on Luke 21 and other passages of Scripture, that didn't seem right to us. In the end, general thanks to everyone who had given seemed the most appropriate response, because we had no way of knowing for sure whether it came easily to some to give £1,000 and was an incredible sacrifice for others to give £10. The amount itself cannot be what we value, because it's not what God values. What counts is the faith being expressed.

The purpose of this chapter isn't to say to the middle classes, 'Hey, your faith isn't as good or as real as the faith of those who have less than you.' Not at all. The point is that we can learn so much through the faith of those who live their lives unable to put their security in wealth or possessions or assets. But it can require intentional effort on our part. We need to humble ourselves and soberly assess our own lives. We can do this by asking ourselves (and those who know us well) some simple questions, such as:

- How am I living by faith currently?
- Which areas of my life require faith at the moment?
- What faith adventure is God inviting me to go on at the moment?
- How can I deliberately stretch my faith?

For those readers who, like me, were once familiar with having less but now have more than enough, it is good to remind ourselves of the faith we exercised by necessity in the past, and to explore with God how we can keep exercising faith with our material wealth even if we are now living comfortably.

I look back at when I was a new Christian and I wanted to take a year out to serve in a church, and I can call to mind the faith that was required to save up enough money to make that possible. I poured a great deal of energy into praying for God's provision, and I had great stories of how God answered those prayers. Likewise, in my mid- to late twenties, when I was overwhelmed with debt, I earnestly sought God over several years for his help to become debt free.

My testimony from that period of my life is that God did two miraculous things. First of all, he taught me to be a good steward and to handle money well. (Please note: those who have less are often much more aware of where every penny of their money goes than those who are comfortable or rich. In my case, I did not know how to budget or handle money well, but many people who are familiar with poverty or 'just about managing' handle their finances exceptionally well.) Second, I became debt free much faster than appeared to be possible on paper. I didn't receive anonymous money through the letterbox, but my debt was cleared inexplicably quickly compared to the rate at which it was assessed that I could repay it.

These days, I have a mortgage on a flat and I am the chief executive of a national charity. I no longer have to watch every penny I spend. Whereas I used to own cars held together by duct tape or at constant risk of the exhaust falling off, my current car is only three years old and the biggest problem with it so far has been a split windscreen wiper. But I don't want my financial faith adventures to be a thing of the past! I am regularly challenged by the faith stories of those who have less than I do, as well as by my own experiences in the past.

Today, I have a choice. Will I make radical decisions to do with generosity, sharing with others, giving and so on, that stretch my faith because they require God to come through for me? Will I imitate the faith of my friends who have less, be inspired by them, honour their faith and obedience, and learn from them?

4

Communication

How we communicate is obviously very important. We want to be understood; most of us want to be appreciated and liked. Even talking about class and the differences between classes brings a risk of misunderstanding and the potential to cause offence. The fact is, working-class people and middle-class people speak very different 'languages'.

The way we talk – our vocabulary and tone – the clothes we wear, how we relate to those in positions of authority, even what we define as success, are all shaped by our class. And because of those many indicators, we are constantly communicating our class position to those around us. Our social class shapes our everyday interactions, from casual exchanges in the pub to how we come across in more formal or institutional settings.

On the penultimate weekend of the 2020 Tokyo Olympics (postponed until 2021 because of the Covid-19 pandemic), Lord Digby Jones commented on Twitter that BBC television presenter Alex Scott had spoiled the coverage of the Games owing to her inability to pronounce her Gs at the end of words. He went on to comment that she needed elocution lessons.[1]

Scott's response via Twitter was very clear: 'I'm from a working class family in East London, Poplar, Tower Hamlets & I am PROUD. Proud of the young girl who overcame obstacles, and proud of my accent! It's me, it's my journey, my grit.' She continued, 'A quick one to any young kids who may not have a certain kind of privilege in life. Never allow judgments on your class, accent or appearance hold you back.'[2] Scott is an accomplished television presenter, yet Lord Jones said that his enjoyment of the Games was spoiled because he didn't like her working-class accent.

It was George Bernard Shaw who said, 'It is impossible for an Englishman to open his mouth without making some other Englishman hate or despise him.'[3]

Accents

One of the most recognizable indicators of social class in the UK is our accent. Ours ears are well attuned to pick up verbal cues. The moment someone opens his or her mouth we instantly, instinctively, make a judgement about that person. In my experience, our accent can affect how we are received and perceived in a church community.

One example of this is when I (Paul) was training some church-based children's workers and they were amazed at how I spoke. They asked how I had learnt my accent, because they assumed I was putting it on to reach children from deprived communities.

Natalie has had similar experiences. For example, a few months after applying to do a Christian leadership training course, she found out that the interviewer had assumed she would not contribute much to the course – based solely on her accent. When, midway through the interview, he asked what else she would be doing while working part-time for the church, and she told him about studying for her master's degree in Political Communication, apparently he nearly fell off his chair. He was shocked that someone who sounded like her would be studying at such a high level.

I remember when I first crossed the threshold of a church as a 25-year-old with no Christian experience or understanding. I was nervous – a foreigner in a strange land! Then my ears tuned in to a comforting voice. I heard someone who spoke like me! It was more welcoming than all the warm words that greeted me going into what was then a peculiar place.

Accents say so much about us. They say where we are from, and maybe to some that we should go back there! They hint at our upbringing and the families who formed us. And our accent will instantly place us in a social hierarchy with our hearers.

A friend of ours who has become well respected for publicly sharing prophetic insights that have a habit of coming to pass, was once told that if she wanted to be taken seriously in this context, she should tone down her accent.

A recent study by Queen Mary University of London found that when people were asked for their opinions of simple accent labels such as 'Cockney' or 'Birmingham English', they tended to penalize non-standard working-class and ethnic accents and uphold middle-class 'standard' speech as the most prestigious.[4]

But we need to realize that accent is not the only communication barrier between the classes.

Watch your words

'Middle-class people are two-faced,' was the immediate answer I got from a working-class lady in my church to the question, 'What do you think about middle-class people?'

Is she right? I don't think so. In my experience, middle-class people are no more two-faced than people from any other background, but I know what she means.

I observed at close hand the misunderstanding and resulting conflict between two 70-year-olds. One was a well-heeled middle-class trustee of a local charity; the other a tough, working-class employee of the same organization. The conversations between them often verged on the farcical. It was one of the most blatant and obvious clashes of class culture I've encountered when it comes to communication.

Let me explain. The working-class employee was always brutally honest in everything he said. If he thought it, he'd invariably say it. He didn't seem at all concerned that he might cause offence, because honesty was a very important trait to him. However, what was important to the middle-class trustee was to not cause offence. He was much more measured in his choice of words, being very careful not to be offensive.

The result was that both men felt insulted by the other.

The middle-class man's careful choice of words, generally chosen so as not to cause offence, had the opposite effect because he was then perceived to be a liar and two-faced. And the working-class man was thought to be downright rude because he *did* say what he thought!

Who was right in this situation? This isn't really a question of right and wrong. The point here is that we understand that different people from different backgrounds and life experience will communicate in very different ways. And when we grasp the truth of that, we will have taken huge strides in our ability to communicate more effectively with a wider spectrum of people – people who have had a very different life experience from our own. And in a church setting, for example, we will be able to receive teaching from someone without making an instinctive judgement about their ability based on whether they pronounce their Gs or not.

Not just words

In certain settings, society encourages us to project a particular image. We're often told that first impressions are important. If you were going for a job interview or maybe meeting your future in-laws for the first time, you'd usually think about what you were going to wear. You would iron your shirt, clean your shoes and ensure your hair wasn't a mess because you would want to communicate something to the people you were meeting. Most of us would want to be seen as amiable and attractive, confident and competent. As you walk into the room you want people to think, 'He's the right one for my daughter,' or, 'That person looks a good fit for this job!'

Why do people do that?

Because we all take subtle cues about social and economic status from the clothes people wear, their hairstyle and their body language, and we subconsciously make an instant value judgement about that person: 'She's got leadership potential,' or, 'Watch him, he's a bit dodgy!'

We also do it with accents. In fact, there are a number of ways in which we subconsciously judge someone's social status based on our first impression of them. This is especially true in western society, where we are conditioned to believe that ability is associated with social status.

This non-verbal communication and placing people in a hierarchy is going on all the time and adds yet another barrier to the challenges faced by working-class people coming into the church and finding acceptance and friendship.

What does the Bible say about this?

Suppose someone comes into your meeting dressed in fancy clothes and expensive jewelry, and another comes in who is poor and dressed in dirty clothes. If you give special attention and a good seat to the rich person, but you say to the poor one, 'You can stand over there, or else sit on the floor' – well, doesn't this discrimination show that your judgments are guided by evil motives?
(Jas. 2.2–4 NLT)

Do you give the well-dressed, confident visitor to your church all the attention and ignore the unkempt young man who crept in at the back of the meeting? A number of years ago, a Methodist minister in North Wales put his congregation to the test. How would they respond to someone who was poor and in dirty clothes? One Sunday, he disguised himself as a homeless drinker. He went without shaving for a few days, put on a wig and a battered old hat, wore faded clothes bought from a charity shop and splashed himself liberally with lager from the can he was holding.

Getting into the church proved much more difficult than I anticipated. Those on 'welcome' duty looked daggers at me and sent me scurrying away in an effort to protect their cars from a man who was clearly trying to steal them, even if he couldn't stand upright for long. Eventually I got as far as the entrance of the church. Behind a glass screen I saw for the first time the care and compassion in the eyes of some of those present – as well as some expressions that led me to question the purpose of this place.

About 20 minutes into the service, I began to bring the drama to a climax. During a hymn, I shuffled forwards to the front of the church. I felt every eye burning into me. When I finally removed my hat and wig, the sigh of relief was audible. It was followed by spontaneous applause. Without having to speak a word, I had managed to communicate a deep message: we all look different on the outside, but on the inside we are essentially the same, needing love, acceptance and fellowship.[5]

We must understand that walking into a church for the first time is a scary, intimidating experience for a lot of people. Over the entrance of my church building is a sign that says 'Welcome' in bright, bold letters. And we mean it – people are very welcome, whoever they are and whatever their age or background. However, we don't want to write 'Welcome' over the door and then, because of our words and actions, inadvertently say, 'You're not welcome!' We have to be very aware of how we communicate with people, and we won't do this in the same way for everyone, as it will depend on what class they are from.

Our church used to do that thing that a lot of churches do: at some point in the service we'd say something like, 'Turn to someone near you, say hello and introduce yourself.' At that point, what most of us do is to begin asking questions.

My brother-in-law Glenn (you'll hear more of his story in a later chapter) came from a very chaotic working-class background. He described the first time he walked into a church service:

> I wasn't culturally prepared for my first experience of a church meeting. First of all, I was disturbed to see men hugging each other. None of the men I knew did that. And second, people kept asking all sorts of intrusive personal questions; was it church or a police convention?

In his previous experience, it was the police and those in authority who asked those intrusive questions, and people like Glenn wouldn't usually trust those in authority. Those people talking to Glenn probably thought they were connecting with him, making him welcome as a first-time visitor to church, when in fact their questioning resulted in him feeling disturbed and alienated by their behaviour.

'Where do you live?' 'Are you married?' 'What do you do?'

Asking questions like these may seem perfectly reasonable, but in fact it can put people off. We need to be willing to adapt the way we communicate to be more inclusive. I think it's best to move away from asking personal questions to start a conversation. Chatting about neutral subjects is far less intrusive, especially with those from a background similar to Glenn's. Don't be an interrogator; be a friend, and make it as easy as possible for all people to feel at home and welcomed.

The quintessentially British conversation opener is, of course, the weather, but you could also chat about a current news item or football or what people are doing over the summer or for Christmas. These are all good starting points for general conversation without being personal or threatening. Finding common ground is an important way of connecting with someone, especially if they are from a different class from you. For example, if you've chatted about your family's new dog and you find out that they too are a dog owner, you've made a genuine connection.

These non-threatening ways of connecting mean that at some point later, people may feel safer about volunteering more personal information, if appropriate.

Learning a new language

In her entertaining and enlightening book, anthropologist Gillian Evans refers to her own journey of discovery as a self-confessed posh person sharing her life with working-class people and talks about learning cross-cultural conversation skills:

Even though we all apparently speak English, it takes me a long time before I can confidently strike up a conversation, know how to greet people properly, what to talk about and how to make a joke and have a laugh in a new and different way. Unlearning what it means to be posh is a slow and excruciating process because it means undoing the value judgement that talking proper implies in relation to common speech. I realise that the educated and expensive talk of the middle-classes is useless to me with [my working-class friend] Sharon; I no longer need to demonstrate how knowledgeable I am about the world, how broad and diverse my experience of it is and how ambitious I am to get on in life and improve myself. When I resort to such talk I am teased mercilessly about being posh and I quickly learn to keep the diversity and breadth of my education and experience firmly in the background of everyday interactions. I need only to focus on the essential business of everyday life: my family's welfare, our health (conversations about the vagaries of the unruly body predominate), work and ways to get money, housework, the drama of relationships, shopping, sex, and gossip about my own and other people's troubles. As long as I can talk about what seem to be the fundamental things in life and demonstrate that I can share stories about often-insurmountable difficulties, which I can also laugh about, then that is all that matters to Sharon.[6]

If we really want to reach the working-class communities of the UK, then we need to learn to communicate effectively. We need to engage with 'those people' and learn their 'language'. We would do well to find out about their closely held values, to discover and learn to appreciate what they hold dear. And, above all, to value them as people – not as projects.

I strongly believe that we need to completely change our mindset so that we can allow ALL people to enrich us as individuals and as churches. We should intentionally allow the culture of a people group that has typically had to overcome far more of life's difficulties than the average middle-class person to enhance our lives.

5

Hospitality

A couple of years ago, I (Natalie) was fed by friends for 46 days in a row. I was pretty open about it as it was happening, which seemed to fuel it as some of my friends wanted to be involved!

When I had mentioned during a talk at a church in Cambridge that the previous year I had inadvertently gone 17 days of being fed by friends, I got a round of applause! In response, I said that maybe I should aim for a whole month of being cooked for by others. Although I was joking, I decided that if I ever noticed I was getting close to matching the 17 days again, I would see how long I could string it out for. So during my 46-day stint, I shared about it publicly on social media as it was going on.

It was interesting to see people's reactions. Some of my friends were astonished at my ability to collect dinner invitations; others marvelled at my audacity in inviting myself to people's homes. A few people made it clear that they considered me to be 'scrounging' – one even took to calling me a 'scrounger' repeatedly during that season.

It didn't bother me, because the hospitality I experienced during those 46 days communicated some profound truths to me about God's love for me, the importance of eating together and the Father's heart for us to welcome people in. As person after person and family after family cooked for me and ate with me, I experienced a deep sense of community and belonging. I experienced church as family in a fresh way.

Hospitality is a vital part of the gospel. Christians are those who have been welcomed into the family of God, not because of any merit or status, ability or impressiveness on our part, but simply because God loves us, is merciful to us and draws us into his family.

Dinner invitations

My new-found faith brought with it kind dinner invitations – a novel concept to me. I don't remember my parents ever going to dinner at anyone's home at 7.30 on a weekday evening. But, embracing this new form of hospitality, after arriving at Christian o'clock, I would soon be invited to help myself from the dishes neatly set out on the table before me. 'After you. You're the guest,' the lovely hosts would say to me, and I would feel anxiety rise within because I didn't know what to do. Before I became a Christian, I had never seen food served in different dishes – a plate of meat, a bowl of vegetables, a dish of potatoes and so on. 'Are you supposed to serve the food on to your plate in a particular order?' I wondered. (I still wonder!) 'How much do you take so that you look grateful but not greedy?'

Dinner invitations were a new experience for me when I joined a church. Though I felt out of my depth and was acutely aware that I didn't know how to behave, I still began to experience something of what it meant to be part of the family of God through the hospitality I was shown.

What I didn't realize at the time was that I was drawing conclusions about hospitality that were very narrow, and not the whole story. I started to equate hospitality with invitations to dinner at a set time, in a set format – namely that it looked like arriving at 7.30 p.m. with a bottle of wine, and probably leaving by 10 p.m., though I am still never quite sure when I'm supposed to leave, and I haven't yet (in more than 25 years) been able to figure out how I am supposed to tell.

It is not that there is anything wrong with that version of hospitality, but simply that it is not the only way. If we want people from all walks of life to feel they belong in our church families, it is helpful to broaden our understanding of key 'ways of doing things', such as the way we extend hospitality and receive it.

Open homes

I adopted the middle-class habit of hospitality, thinking it was 'the Christian way' of welcoming people into our homes. After becoming a Christian, for many years I thought about hospitality in this very limited way I had learnt from church. But in the last few years, as I have started to reflect on my upbringing more, I have realized that I knew and experienced a very different form of hospitality when I was a child.

After we lived in a sixteenth-floor flat, with some help from the council we were able to move into a small, three-bedroom, terraced house. The row of houses was set between a main road and a railway track, with the signal box for the trains directly in front of our home, cutting off the road into a dead-end. I would never have called this hospitality at the time – and neither would anyone on our street – but today I think that is the most accurate word for how we lived alongside our neighbours. Everyone would walk straight into each other's homes. The kitchens were at the front and the living rooms at the back, so it was completely normal to help yourself to a snack and a drink before you went through to the lounge and said hello to the person or people who lived there. You could stay as long as you liked – I can't remember anyone ever asking me to go home!

In fact, when I was writing this chapter, I asked a friend who lives in social housing on a local estate to describe what hospitality looks like for her, and she said, 'You're welcome to come over any time. Walk in. If I'm busy, you can hang out in my house while I carry on. If I need to go out, I'll leave you there until I come back. You can help yourself to whatever. If I need you to go for some reason, I'll tell you to go.' To me, this is the hospitality I knew as a child, but it feels increasingly rare in my life today.

A contrasting example that also happened while I was writing this chapter is that one of my other friends invited people over who significantly outstayed their welcome, but she wouldn't have dreamed of telling them for fear of being impolite or hurting their feelings. This invisible divide between prioritizing politeness (no matter how inauthentic) and prioritizing honesty (no matter how harsh) has already been explored in the previous chapter on communication.

Most of my working-class friends would not invite someone over for dinner, but they would have an open door to you at all times. If you turn up and you are hungry, they will make sure they feed you, even if it's with the last of the food they have in their home.

The moment that I realized I had disregarded what I had experienced as a child as hospitality, and instead had come to see more formal dinner invitations as the only expression of it, came when a friend turned up unexpectedly at my flat. When my buzzer rang one evening, my first thought was an irritated, 'Who's that?' Then, when we started speaking through the intercom and I found out it was a close friend, my natural inclination was to ask what she wanted, rather than to invite her up. In fact, she had to ask to come in. She said, 'Aren't you going to let me in?' Even after I buzzed her in through the main door, when she arrived at the door to my flat I was still confused about why she had turned up unannounced. Again, she said, 'Nat, what's wrong with you? Invite me inside!'

Hospitality looks very different across the classes (and across different ethnic groups as well), and as we saw with faith, there are undoubtedly some lessons that those who are middle class could learn from those who are or identify as working class. (Lessons can be learnt by both groups, but many of us default to automatically assuming that the working classes can learn from the middle classes, so here I am just seeking to redress the balance.) When we understand our differences, we can embrace them, learn from them and enjoy them.

Welcoming all

The Bible says we need to be careful not to 'neglect to show hospitality to strangers' (Heb. 13.2 ESV UK), and biblical hospitality seems to involve not just welcoming people into our homes at predetermined times and dates that are convenient for us (as lovely as that can be), but really inviting people in to do life with us.

The hospitality shown to me by my working-class neighbours when I was still at school, and by my working-class friends now, allows me to disrupt their routines. They don't set parameters on their welcome. That might sit uncomfortably for many of us, but it is also what we see demonstrated in the life of Jesus, and in the church in the New Testament. What's more, the model set before us by Jesus and his disciples reveals that true hospitality isn't just about when we will welcome people in, but also who we welcome.

Jesus ate with a wide range of people, often inviting himself into people's homes. The religious people around him were often shocked by the people he would share meals with. The Pharisees asked his disciples, 'Why does your teacher eat with tax collectors and sinners? (Matt. 9.11). For Jesus to sit at a table with Matthew the tax collector and his friends would have been shocking. Matthew was a Jewish tax collector – he collected money from his own people, the Jewish community, for the Romans, who were their oppressive enemy. It is likely that he would have topped up the amount he collected so that he could earn more, as was customary at the time. Tax collectors were hated by the Jewish community. They were thought of as thieves and traitors, stealing from their own people.

Matthew himself was wealthy – we can tell that from the fact that his home was large enough to throw a banquet for many people to recline at the table with Jesus. It would have been offensive to many for Jesus to invite Matthew to follow him. Jesus surrounding himself with fishermen might have made some sense – people earning an honest living, working hard, people we might call 'the salt of the earth' types – but for Jesus to associate with and even befriend the most despised people of the day would have been outrageous.

Jesus did not hold Matthew at arm's length. He didn't make him clean up his act before he would spend time in his home. He welcomed him as he was. Jesus didn't have a home to invite Matthew to (Matt. 8.20), but he demonstrated hospitality – radical inclusivity and acceptance – by eating with Matthew in Matthew's own home. As one commentator writes:

> For Jesus and his disciples to eat with such people was scandalous; it meant they were accepting these tax collectors and identifying with them and sinners. Yet this characterised Jesus' ministry . . . The criticism was natural, as they were rendering themselves unclean and violators of the Torah by their association with such people.[1]

It would have been just as scandalous to the religious people of Jesus' day for him to eat with Simon the leper (Mark 14.3).

But I don't think Jesus upset only the religious leaders with his giving and receiving of hospitality. Some of us find it easy to love Jesus for sitting down to eat with 'sinners', those who were sick or poor, prostitutes, tax collectors, those no one cared about. When we see Jesus expressing mercy and compassion to people such as this, many of us are moved and grateful that he mixed with the lowly and despised. However, he also ate with those who were doing the despising: Jesus went into the homes of various Pharisees on a number of occasions too (see Luke 7.36; 11.37; 14.1). If I am honest, I like this Jesus who ate with people like me, but I am not so keen on the idea of Jesus eating with those who exploited people or looked down on them.

When considering our own hospitality, it is worth thinking about who we will eat with. Whatever our own background, will we eat with people from very different walks of life from our own? Will we adapt our form of hospitality to suit people with different customs and habits? If we are willing to do this, it might make us uncomfortable while we prioritize someone else's comfort. For example, since I started telling my story about how I had never seen food set out in dishes and did not really know if there were any unspoken rules when it came to serving myself, some of my friends make a point of dishing up my plate of food for me, so as to not put me in that unfamiliar situation. With some friends, I know that if we are going to eat together, they would prefer to go to somewhere simple and inexpensive, maybe a fast-food outlet, a café or a pub, rather than invite me into their home or come to mine.

No strings attached

It is important not to expect our hospitality to be reciprocated in the same way that we extend it to others. My mum, for example, would not contemplate hosting someone in her home for a meal at the moment. There is nothing wrong with her place, but she is house-proud and would feel too ashamed to have people come inside. She feels this so strongly that I don't think more than one or two of her friends from outside her street have ever been inside her home in the last decade. She would be mortified if she were expected to have someone over for a dinner party, not least because she doesn't have a dining room or even a dining table.

Jesus even mentioned that we shouldn't expect to be repaid for our hospitality, when he said:

When you give a dinner or a banquet, do not invite your friends or your brothers or your relatives or rich neighbours, lest they also invite you in return and you be repaid. But when you give a feast, invite the poor, the crippled, the lame, the blind, and you will be blessed, because they cannot repay you. (Luke 14.12–14)

Along similar lines, one of the greatest examples of hospitality that I have received in the church has been friends and pastors inviting me into their homes on special occasions, such as Christmas or significant birthdays. Including others in these events that are seen in much of the western world as 'family times' – times to hunker down in our own households to the exclusion of others – can be a precious and healing expression of care for those who are isolated, vulnerable or feel left out or as if they don't fit in.

Prior to the coronavirus pandemic, I volunteered at a local night shelter for a few winters in a row. Most often, I would do a breakfast shift before work, but occasionally I would pick up an evening shift. When I did that, the best part was sitting down together for a meal – there was something very levelling about guests and volunteers eating at a shared table. It was the one part of the evening where, if anyone walked into the room, they would not be able to tell which of us were volunteers and who were the guests. I wonder if it was meals like this that Jesus was hoping the Pharisees could experience when he told them to invite those who couldn't repay them for a meal.

Hospitable churches

It is good for us to reflect on hospitality in our churches, as well as in our homes. Jackie Pullinger is the well-known author of *Chasing the Dragon*, a book about her experiences in Hong Kong of seeing gang members and drug lords come to faith in Jesus and be delivered from their addictions, violent tempers and so on. From her decades of experience, Jackie points out that people can tell when we are happy to share the church's food with them, but wouldn't share our own.[2] It might be provoking for us to reflect on this – especially those of us who are heavily involved in social action projects such as food banks. Would we sit down for a meal with those we are serving and supporting outside the confines of a church-based project? Or are projects a helpful way to do good to people 'not like us' while keeping them held firmly at arm's length?

Most of us who are committed to local churches want to know that they are hospitable and welcoming to newcomers, but even in this, there are different expressions. What is welcoming to one person might not be to someone else. One of my co-author Paul's working-class friends said that she was initially put off church when she came along as a non-Christian, because church members wouldn't let her sit in the background for a few weeks. She wanted to sneak in and sneak out. She didn't want to be 'welcomed' in the way that many of us think to welcome visitors. Partly, she was worried about being asked three questions: 'Where do you live?'; 'What do you do?'; 'Where are you going on holiday?' These were the sorts of questions she was asked in casual conversations with people who were trying to be hospitable, but instead of making her feel welcome, they made her feel uncomfortable.

Several of my working-class friends find church small groups and dinner invitations 'a bit odd'. Midweek small groups can cause significant anxiety to people who are not familiar with going to people's houses in this way. As one friend said to Paul and me while we were researching this book, 'I wouldn't phone someone after 7 p.m., let alone go to their house! I wouldn't sit at a table to eat. I don't know when I'm supposed to leave. I'd rather go to the pub, or meet outside a home.'

I have heard several stories of people being invited for a meal and asking, 'Why?' In one case, when a church leader invited a couple who were new to the church over for dinner, the couple asked, 'Why? What have we done?'

Our church events can be similarly alienating, albeit unintentionally. One friend of ours said, 'Evangelistic events that involve a meal never serve pie and peas, for example. And the events themselves are never working-class social events such as bingo. We want hospitality, but churches do entertainment. You want to pull me out of my environment to come to your event or show.'

At Paul's church, they hosted a very successful evangelistic event that fitted working-class culture: they set up a boxing ring in their hall and while people were watching the boxing, they were served chicken and chips in a basket. It was followed by a testimony from one of the boxers. Interestingly, the first time Paul ever suggested an evangelistic boxing event (at a different church), he was told it was 'not something appropriate for a church to do'.

Hospitality is not primarily something that happens in our homes or our churches, but in our hearts. You don't even need to use your home to show hospitality, because hospitality is more to do with your attitude than whether you invite someone round and give them dinner. When Paul's son was three or four years old, he offered his doughnut – which was a special treat from his dad – to a stranger they were talking to on the beach. That's hospitality.

More recently, I sat down with a guy who was begging on the street. At the end of our conversation, he said how much he had appreciated me sitting beside him, talking to him at eye level, because he said most contact he had with passers-by involved them looking down at him as they stood above him. A simple act of sitting down on the street became hospitality.

When we are using our homes, it is not just about how much we invite people in, but also how much we keep people out. In British middle-class culture, increasingly our homes are treated as our own. They are our safe places, our little castles. But God is inviting us to be increasingly hospitable – even to strangers, whereby we may even be entertaining angels, unaware (see Heb. 13.2). To do this, we might need to rethink whether our approach is *the* way to do hospitality, or just *one* way to do it, and therefore we may need to learn from and imitate those around us, looking not for the best practical way to demonstrate hospitality, but the best way to ensure that true hospitality is something we really value.

6

Money and generosity

'She'd give you her last tenner, she would.'

You may have heard words similar to these spoken to affirm that someone is sacrificially generous. It's saying that even though she doesn't have much, she will willingly give what she has for the benefit of someone else.

The Bible seems to support this attitude to giving.

Jesus sat down near the collection box in the Temple and watched as the crowds dropped in their money. Many rich people put in large amounts. Then a poor widow came and dropped in two small coins.

Jesus called his disciples to him and said, 'I tell you the truth, this poor widow has given more than all the others who are making contributions. For they gave a tiny part of their surplus, but she, poor as she is, has given everything she had to live on.'
(Mark 12.41–44 NLT)

And elsewhere we read:

Don't store up treasures here on earth . . . Look at the birds. They don't plant or harvest or store food in barns, for your heavenly Father feeds them. And aren't you far more valuable to him than they are?
(Matt. 6:19, 26 NLT)

Take a lesson from the ants, you lazybones . . .
they labour hard all summer,

gathering food for the winter.
(Prov. 6.6–8 NLT)

We have a bit of a dilemma: the Bible seems to have two contradictory teachings when it comes to wealth and possessions. In Matthew 6 we're encouraged not to accumulate wealth. And in the book of Proverbs we're urged to put aside for the future. There seems to be a balance between being wise with what we have and not living in fear of not having enough – we're to be good stewards *and* trust God for his provision of all we need.

Different attitudes

When it comes to attitudes to money and generosity, you can often see clear differences between the classes. We need to learn and be challenged by each other and see that, just because we have different attitudes, neither is necessarily right or wrong.

When I (Paul) was young, I used to think well-off people were 'tight' with their money. As a teenager, during the school holidays I would often help out at my family's builders' merchants. I would work alongside my dad, loading lorries with various building materials. We'd then drive to the client's property and unload the bricks, bags of cement and various building materials by hand. It was often hard physical work. Before we set off, I would always look at the delivery address on the customer's invoice. If we were going to one of the more exclusive, expensive properties in areas like Chislehurst and Bickley, my heart would sink a little. Why? Because I'd learnt from experience that the people in the big posh houses would never give you a tip! I would always prefer to go to the modest council houses because those tenants would invariably recognize your hard work by being generous. 'There you go, son; that's for you, treat yerself!' they would say as they put a folded banknote in your hand.

My schoolboy experience of working-class generosity is backed up by academic research.

According to a study from the Queen Mary University of London,[1] people with less are likely to give more. Researchers set up an economic experiment where people were labelled as either 'low status' or 'high status' in terms of social, economic and educational attainment and told to contribute any amount of money they wanted into a group pot that would later be divided among all the participants.

The so called 'lower status' individuals always contributed more to the pot.

It seems that our social standing can impact our social behaviour; our attitude to money is shaped in some way by our class.

In the first volume of his insightful and furiously funny autobiography, working-class broadcaster and writer Danny Baker talks candidly about his attitude to money:

I am from totally non-moneyed roots, where the idea of having any savings was unimaginable – wasteful, even . . . I have always regarded even the most rudimentary financial planning as the dreary stamp of a sluggard. In our family you earned money, you got paid, you knocked it out. You spent it on your kids, on friends, on noisy nights and rollicking days. Most importantly, you went through it before anyone could ask for it back or produce something as sordid as a utility bill. When they did, you told them to f*** off until you had moved a few things about. My dad and his brothers all talked openly of being flush or being 'pot-less' — and with equal indifference.

Baker continues:

Nothing I have done in my career has ever been to amass wealth. Even today, I have no second or holiday home, no top-of-the-range car, less than ten grand in the bank – often much less! Yet I have stayed in the presidential suite at the Four Seasons New York, flown Concorde, and had lots of six-week holidays with people I love – and I have paid for it all myself. Every penny I have earned and it has been millions – has been used to facilitate a wonderful series of experiences or otherwise to foot the bill for something extended, rash and marvellous.[2]

In many ways, my views resonate with Danny Baker's. Is that because of similarities in our upbringing? I've certainly learnt how to be content in all circumstances, to have the same attitude whether I'm 'flush' or 'pot-less'.

There are lessons in the Bible for all of us – in some ways the encouragement to all people is the same: don't be preoccupied with money and possessions. For those who have a lot, don't set your hope on it. For those who have little, know that God cares about your needs and will provide.

My finances are comparatively healthy right now, but as a Christian I have had times of genuine hardship. There was a time when there was a severe slump in the building industry. The company I was working for had no more work on the books and was forced to lay me off. With a young family to provide for, I was suddenly forced to rely on the minimal amount available through the benefits system.

We trusted God; we had faith that he wouldn't let us down. And we learnt huge lessons about trusting God for provision, just as we saw in the earlier chapter on faith. One time we had to do a week's grocery shopping for a family of six with just £15! We were only able to buy a few staples: some bread, milk and potatoes and not much more. When we got home from the supermarket, we found that someone had put some cash through the letter box, enough to buy food for the week. We got straight back in the car and went to do a proper shop!

Generous with a little

Even with the little we had in those times, we chose to continue being as generous as we could. We couldn't save. We lived hand to mouth, but we were determined to share meals with people and to help neighbours who were in even greater financial need than us. Those experiences gave me a real insight into life on the dole; how emotionally draining it can be and how inventive you must be to survive. Times of financial hardship forced us to draw closer to God every day – that's a good thing, but it can also be very hard work. If you are constantly juggling such a small amount of money, it can cost you emotionally. You've got to admire people who have to survive solely on benefits.

There was a time that an open-handed attitude to money resulted in an amazing blessing!

When our children were young, a family we knew kindly offered us their home for a two-week holiday while they were away on their summer vacation. By this time, I was working full-time for the church. Every penny was budgeted and accounted for. There was no slack in the family finances for things as extravagant as a holiday. So this offer was a real blessing.

In the months leading up to the break, we excitedly put aside the money to spend on our holiday by the sea. The day was approaching, the bags were being packed and the kids were drawing pictures of the things they planned to do on the beach. Then, the evening before we were to load up our old VW van with children and suitcases and all the paraphernalia of a perfect seaside holiday, my wife suddenly said, 'When I was praying, God told me we should give all our holiday money away!'

'What? All of it? Are you sure?'

'Yes, all of it!'

All our hard-earned, hard-saved holiday money was going to be given to someone else!

We prayed and asked who we should give the money to. Again,

God spoke clearly. We put the cash in an envelope and posted it through their letter box late that evening.

Now we hadn't got any money! We were, like Danny Baker said, 'pot-less', properly skint, with nothing in the bank, no savings and the current account at zero! I'd got enough fuel in the van to get us to our destination but not to get us back! Nevertheless, the next morning, we still set off on our summer adventure.

When we arrived at the house, we found that the owners had kindly baked some chocolate brownies as a welcome gift – the kids had those for their evening meal. The next day, we found half a loaf in the freezer, so we breakfasted on toast and then trooped off to the local church. At church, in faith, I expected someone to present us with a wad of cash, saying words like, 'God has seen your obedience and has told me to give you this.' Nothing. I told the kids to have as many church biscuits as they wanted!

After the Sunday service, we returned to the holiday home, but the children wanted to go out and do exciting holiday things. So at that point we explained what had happened and that we all needed to pray.

We spent some time praying and worshipping together, and then it happened . . .

My wife walked out into the hallway, and there, on the mat by the front door, was an envelope with both our names neatly written on it. Inside was a load of cash! No one knew our situation. We celebrated the goodness of God together and took the kids out. The holiday had begun!

That was a great lesson. Over the years, we've learnt to trust God for provision.

This attitude to money may seem reckless to some. It may not always be seen as the 'correct' way, but I've found it liberating.

'Wise' stewards

Often, we are encouraged to be wise stewards of our money.

In some ways, I wish the Bible's teaching on saving and financial security was straightforward, but, as we've already seen, it isn't – there are passages where we're encouraged to save for the future and others where we're encouraged to not worry about it. There's nothing wrong with giving all your money away. There's nothing wrong with having nothing. And there's nothing wrong with saving. Churches save. Individuals save. I saved for that holiday. But if you are saving simply to insulate yourself from every eventuality and potential hardship, that's not wise stewardship. That's trusting in wealth before trusting in God. John Wesley preached this: 'Earn as much as you can, save as much as you can, give as much as you can.' This sounds like a healthy balance – but we should also be provoked by how Wesley lived: he gave away the vast majority of what he earnt throughout his life.[3]

There will always be times when a more recklessly generous attitude to money is the right thing to have. There are times when 'wise stewardship' is to give some or even all of it away. We need to be discerning and balance the practicalities of living in the 'here and now' while also living in the light of eternity. We should be constantly asking what God's will is. And then putting it into practice.

What we mustn't do is look down on those who do things differently from us and be tempted to impose our ways on others. In fact, sometimes we can hinder someone's obedience to God by our nervousness about their generosity. If anything, when people around us give extravagantly, we should learn from them and seek to imitate them.

A friend of mine who was on the staff of a church in an affluent town in the UK was strongly encouraged by his fellow leaders to take out a mortgage on a property and not remain in his council-owned home. 'Don't throw your money away on rent, where you will have nothing to show for it. Invest your money in property.' They seemed to see buying a property as wise stewardship.

I was in a conversation about money, housing and the future with a senior church leader. I said to him, 'I've trusted God to provide all through my Christian life and I'll continue to do that in my retirement.'

I was disappointed with his response: 'I've had too many people in my office saying things like that.' He went on to imply, without knowing any of my circumstances, that I should have been a wise steward, that I should have provided for my future with a decent pension and 'invested' in a property.

I now have enough disposable income to enjoy a meal out with my wife, to buy someone a surprise gift or just to give it away to someone who needs it more than me. But for a long time that wasn't my experience. For many years I lived from payday to payday, unable to save if I wanted to. I meet many Christians who just don't get that concept. I've found that so many Christians from a middle-class background genuinely don't understand that there are mature Christians who are in work who live like this, having to budget every penny, every month. I've spoken to middle-class Christian friends who, at the end of the month, say they've got no money, yet I know they've got thousands in savings. What they mean is, there's not much money in their current account. That could cause real tension with other church members who, when they say they've got no money, mean exactly that.

Today, more than ever, people's financial circumstances are very precarious – people working in the gig economy, those in minimum wage jobs and on zero-hour contracts, people in industries so precarious that some could lose their job overnight.

Suddenly there could be many people in our churches who, for whatever reason, will need urgent ongoing financial support. It will then be the responsibility of those of us who have the resources to help them – not to raise an eyebrow in disdain and mutter something about them needing to be better stewards. If there are Christians in financial need among us, surely we should be sharing our resources so that no one is in need (see Acts 2.45; 4.34–35).

There will always be the potential for tension and misunderstanding between the classes over attitudes to money, but whatever our background, whatever we earn, we must all be full of faith and love for others when it comes to money and generosity.

7

Community

When you think of the word 'community', what comes to mind? For me (Natalie), it's the neighbourhood I grew up in as a kid, where we played in the street and walked freely in and out of each other's homes. When I think about my present-day community, church comes to mind – especially the handful of deep friendships with a diverse group of people who love Jesus and encourage me to keep doing the same.

It's often been said about the church: where else do you get young and old, rich and poor, black and white in the same community? We can even be in danger of proudly commending ourselves for this. But the church doesn't have the monopoly on diverse community. When I worked behind the scenes for a local political group, I was surprised to hear them say exactly the same thing about their own group. When people become Christians, do we expect them to leave their community and cleave to the church because we think (whether consciously or subconsciously) that this is where real community is found?

The truth is that churches should be vibrant communities of Christians who are meaningfully involved in each other's lives. In Acts 2.42 (ESV UK), the Bible says all the believers 'devoted themselves to . . . the fellowship'. 'Devoted' is a strong word. It is used by the apostle Paul in Romans 12.10 where he writes, 'Be devoted to one another in love. Honour one another above yourselves.' There are a hundred 'one another' commands in the New Testament, one-third of which are about getting along with each other! For example, 'Accept one another' (Rom. 15.7, sometimes translated 'welcome' or 'receive'), be kind, tender-hearted and forgiving towards one another (Eph. 4.32), and be humble towards one another (1 Pet. 5.5). It is very clear in the Bible that Christians might struggle to get along, but we are called to work hard at it. It's not a pipe dream or an optional extra – the church is supposed to be distinctive from the world around. One of the ways in which the gospel is most powerfully demonstrated is by how diverse people with nothing but Jesus in common love one another. Jesus said that people will know we are his disciples by our love for each other (John 13.35).

When I (Natalie) became a Christian, the importance of church meetings was stressed to me. I was involved in judo at a regional level, but competitions were always on Sundays so I was encouraged by other Christians to give this up, which I did. Looking back on it, I think it was the right decision, but I'm not sure that Sunday attendance is the primary measure of how involved in church community someone is. Some people, when they come to faith, already have a very strong sense of community. We can push them to make the church their primary allegiance, but we need to be careful that they don't burn bridges with their original community. We are not called to pull people away from their networks, but to empower them to live out their faith in the setting in which they're placed: 'Each person should remain in the situation they were in when God called them' (1 Cor. 7.20).

Community means different things to different people. It's worth noting that many experts have found community difficult to define. Sociologists, anthropologists, historians and, of course, politicians of all hues have attempted to define it. In his book *Class in Britain*, historian David Cannadine refers to the idea of 'Middle England', a phrase that gained popularity in political vocabulary after Mrs Thatcher adapted Richard Nixon's rendering: 'Middle America'. 'Middle England' has, for many, come to be shorthand for a certain type of community. Cannadine quotes journalist Martin Jacques: 'Middle England is primarily a political invention . . . a metaphor for respectability, the nuclear family, heterosexuality, conservatism, whiteness, middle-age and the status quo.' Cannadine continues, 'It is, in short, the latest version of the traditional three-layer model of society, which has always privileged those at the centre.'[1]

What is community?

As we've said, community is defined in different ways, often to serve different views. We could look at it as a group of individuals who band together because of a shared interest, such as members of the Women's Institute or the local working men's club. We might talk about the Jewish community or the banking community. Communities connected by a shared characteristic or interest often have nothing much to do with place.

Alternatively, community could be viewed primarily as a geographic area: part of a city, a town, a village or even an estate. It is very common for individuals to find their identity through affinity with a place. The thing that people have in common is where they live. But it's not simply living in a place. Place can then be overlaid with shared experience; the repeated connections with others from the locality can strengthen community. In many areas, supporting the local football team will be a focus of a shared community identity. Local pubs may not be as popular as they once were, but they are still a focal point for many. Schools, especially primary schools, which typically have a very local catchment area, are also places where people connect around both geography and a shared experience. These are some of the contexts where we can connect with local people.

Sometimes it's only when we hear other people talk about what community means to them that we can see how different their experiences might be. Here is how one family related to me (Paul) has connected with their community.

Jake and Sara's story

Jake and Sara have both been Christians since they were teenagers. Now in their early thirties, they live with their four children in a two-bedroom council flat in south London, close to Tower Bridge. Jake has been a firefighter for a decade after doing various jobs in the building industry. Until very recently, Sara was a full-time mum and homemaker.

When asked how they care for the people in their community, Jake said, 'We've had our roots put down in this area; we've spent our whole lives here. Caring for our community has always been about living life alongside people.'

He went on to give examples of different community contexts where lasting friendships have been made: at their children's school, as a member of the local amateur boxing club, church community outreach activities like kids' clubs and play groups. These are some of the environments where they make friends and connect with their community.

How do they develop those friendships, with a family of four young children and a demanding job working shifts as a firefighter? 'We've always had an open-door policy at our flat. We've been very open, sharing our lives, living our lives with people and not showing any judgement; being honest about our own flaws and issues, which means that people then feel open to share their own feelings and flaws with us, often over food. We've helped people with relationship issues or housing issues, which can sometimes be quite complex. At that point you've got a decision to make: "Am I going to help that person or not?" We've always tried to make the decision to commit, and that hasn't always been easy, but it's always amazed me how blown away people are by the support and time we've given them.'

Interestingly, they don't seem to have many time restrictions on when they are available to the community around them. People turn up at their door unannounced at random hours. They always make themselves available for advice, emotional and practical support, or even just to share a meal. I wondered about the impact on their four children, ranging in age from 13 to seven. They all share in this open-door attitude, they are all very gregarious and confident when talking with adults.

Sara pointed out that they've always kept it very natural, believing that God has said he will bring across their path the people he wants them to invest in. 'We've never really sought people out; we've just been friendly. It's not like we've gone out looking for people.' They certainly haven't set up a project, they haven't established a charity or a church plant. They have just lived life in their local community.

When you talk with Jake and Sara, you don't get any sense of 'We know best'; there's no hint of a saviour mentality. In fact, they candidly talk about their own attitudes and outlook being challenged as they've supported their neighbours and friends. It is obviously important to them both that people feel relaxed and at home when they come to the flat, knowing they're not going to be judged.

What does this community lifestyle look like in practice? 'We often make an extra meal or two in case someone comes round unannounced, or maybe there will be a neighbour who needs some food.' This is really common among working-class neighbourhoods and estates – to make extra food, or to have extra food ready, in case someone turns up unannounced or is in need. Although friends and neighbours have got to know about Jake and Sara's open-door policy and can turn up whenever they please, they have put in some basic boundaries: if the phone rings at mealtime, they don't answer, choosing to focus on the people they are with. They will regularly factor in times away from the flat to recharge – simple things like family time in the park or going for pizza after picking the kids up from school. However, even though they have clear boundaries around their time, Jake stressed that sometimes you must allow yourself to make exceptions and go outside those boundaries.

'A true sign of someone's character,' he said, 'is how they are with people who can't offer them anything in return.' This echoes the words of Jesus mentioned earlier:

> When you give a dinner or a banquet, do not invite your friends or your brothers or your relatives or rich neighbours, lest they also invite you in return and you be repaid. But when you give a feast, invite the poor, the crippled, the lame, the blind, and you will be blessed, because they cannot repay you. For you will be repaid at the resurrection of the just.
> (Luke 14.12–14 ESV UK)

The loss of working-class community

To truly understand how important community is, and how different people understand it, we need to explore how it was formed for the working classes, and their sense of loss over it. Many established communities and towns were built around a large local industry – for example, car construction in places like Coventry or the shoe manufacturing industry of Northampton. Over recent decades, there has been massive economic and social change in communities up and down the UK. In part, that change has come about as a result of the loss of the traditional industries around which towns and communities grew up and developed their own sense of shared identity.

I (Paul) have lived and ministered in the former docking community of Bermondsey for approaching 30 years. When speaking to local people, I hear many of the older residents still lament the loss of the docks and the related industries that grew up around them – employers such as the famous biscuit manufacturer Peek Freans, who in the 1940s employed around 4,000 people largely drawn from the streets immediately surrounding the factory. Everyone in the area knew someone who worked at the Peek Freans factory. The company pioneered medical, dental and eye care for its staff, and had a sports facility. Like other large companies at the time (such as Cadbury), community spirit was part of the fabric of the organization.

That's undoubtedly one of the reasons why the closures of those industries were long lamented. People felt increasingly isolated as what they saw as part of their identity was taken from them. I recall one tragic account of a dock worker who took his own life after the Surrey Docks were closed in 1970. People's sense of identity was often defined by the industries around which those communities grew. The loss of traditional jobs for some was damaging economically, but it also damaged those communities culturally, alongside the loss of the manufacturing base in the UK.

Town planners replaced streets of terraced houses with blocks of flats in the 1960s and 1970s, causing many who had lived there to lament the loss of community. There has also been a rapid erosion of social housing as people have taken the government-offered right to buy their council property at a discount. This has obviously helped some to find stability and be more firmly rooted in the local area. But the truth is that many bought them, then, as soon as they could, either sold to private landlords or became landlords themselves and rented out the properties on a series of short-term lets. This has created very transient populations, which further erodes any sense of community on many estates. In Hastings, where I (Natalie) live, the local council has recognized the negative impact on the town as a whole of transient residents, so it has restricted licences for houses of multiple occupation (HMOs) to two bedrooms. It has done this as an attempt to stop short-term room lets to individual people, in the hope of creating a community of families who will be rooted in the town for the long term.

As individual Christians and churches, we need to be sensitive to issues of cultural change in communities, and to understand that many people feel the impact of issues that many middle-class people have not encountered.

This is my home

A strong sense of community in certain neighbourhoods can mean that outsiders are viewed with suspicion. This is very important to know, particularly if you are moving into an area to start a church, for example. Where a community of people have lived, gone to school, worked and socialized in the same small area, new people moving in are not always automatically welcomed, especially if it coincides with the gentrification of a previously neglected part of town. When amenities are suddenly improved and shops are opened that cater for the middle-class newcomers, it could well be resented.

I (Paul) suppose it's a bit like someone moving into your home and then, after a couple of weeks, you get home from work and they've completely changed the décor in the kitchen and have started to knock down some of the internal walls, telling you that open plan is much better. And then you discover they've replaced the food in your fridge with food you don't eat!

If you are moving into a tight-knit community, it is really important to respect it and understand that you are unlikely to be accepted as part of it overnight. Become part of the community before thinking you can transform it. Acknowledge that you have a lot to learn from the community, rather than thinking you can impose your way of life upon it. It's not about shrinking back from mission, but about being humble.

Whether or not you're moving into a specific community, having respect for the different areas in which people live in your town or city – and the way they do things – is really important. We mustn't be prejudiced towards people based simply on where they live. If people where I (Natalie) live in Hastings hear that someone lives on one of the deprived estates, there is often an automatic assumption about their life, employment, education and situation. There are specific areas that are 'no go' unless you live there. This is true of many communities across the whole country, where value judgements are made by one group of people about another based solely on their postcode.

This is nothing new. In Bob Holman's book *Faith in the Poor*, he describes the media portrayal of life on the huge Easterhouse social housing estate on the outskirts of Glasgow versus the reality he experienced once he moved there. Easterhouse was reported to be a place of squalor and poverty, a broken community where drugs and vandalism were rife. Holman highlights the visit of a journalist from a national newspaper arriving at the airport to cover a story about the intention to arm local police with CS sprays:

> At the airport, he found the taxi driver reluctant to drive to Easterhouse for fear of what would happen to him and the taxi. In actuality, they arrived with no trouble and the reporter was set down in a quiet and pleasant street.

Holman also describes the lack of investment and job opportunities locally and links that to the negative, media-driven image of the area: 'Young people complain that their job applications have less chance because they live in Easterhouse.'[2] This is still the case today: the negative reputation of an area leads to assumptions about the residents and discrimination based on nothing more than where they live.

Other ways we form tribes

Tribalism is rife throughout society. I (Natalie) went to a secondary school that was known as the roughest in town, in one of the most deprived parts of the town. I learnt tribalism from a young age based on two-way prejudices against people who went to other schools. Likewise, when I started going to nightclubs, there was a clear division in Hastings between those who went to The Crypt (typically middle class, academic, 'enlightened' – although somehow I found myself in this group because of my sixth-form friendship circle or 'tribe') and those who went to Saturdays (typically working class, vocational, streetwise). There was huge prejudice between the two groups – our clothing was different (and each hated what the other wore), our taste in music and cinema was different (and we judged each other based on it). Probably the only thing we had in common was our shared dislike and distrust of each other. The Saturdays tribe thought The Crypt lot were pretentious, spoilt and had no clue about real life; The Crypt tribe made disparaging comments about how the other group would drive up teen pregnancy and absent-dad stats in the town.

Sometimes our prejudices are based on fear, but more often than not it is just that we don't understand and value difference. As Christians, we need to work hard to overcome this sort of division and mistrust in our communities. We need to be aware of the tribalism that exists all around us – even within the church – and actively seek to imitate Jesus, who 'destroyed the barrier, the dividing wall of hostility' between groups who previously despised one another (Eph. 2.14).

The truth is that, in our modern society, we can pick and choose which church we go to and only mix with people like us, if we want to. But that is not what we are called to – it is not God's vision or plan for his church. Earlier we saw how Jake and Sara have worked hard to connect with their community and at the same time to introduce people to Jesus and his love. But it is good for us to ask ourselves a challenging question: would their friends and neighbours find community and acceptance in the local church?

Behind that question lies the much deeper issue of whether our churches are set up to reflect the cultural diversity of our communities. For example, where Natalie lives in East Sussex, the population is overwhelmingly white (96 per cent),[3] whereas where I (Paul) live in Southwark, around half of the population are white (54 per cent) and more than 120 languages are spoken, with 11 per cent of households not speaking English as a first language.[4] So we wouldn't expect our churches to look the same. In the same way, if you live in a leafy suburb, you will want to make sure your church is accessible to anyone who lives in a pocket of deprivation in your community, but you wouldn't expect your entire outreach programme to be focused on the working classes or those in poverty. Invisible divides within our churches are much more of a problem when we are located in or close to working-class communities but have set up our meetings and activities to cater only to the middle classes.

So another question to ask is this: is your church a community where people can find love, acceptance, dignity and friendship, whatever their background; whatever their job or level of formal education? Will people who prefer to watch boxing to a box set of *The West Wing* be just as likely to find genuine community within your church?

8

Us and them: attitudes to authority

In the early 2000s, community policing was reinstated – the government wanted to return to the days of a 'bobby on the beat' in every neighbourhood. Smiling, uniformed police officers were employed specifically to connect with their local community. They would develop partnerships with various agencies and generally build relationships with key individuals and community groups.

One morning, two of those community policemen turned up in uniform, unannounced, for a Sunday meeting at my (Paul's) church and sat at the back, waiting for the service to begin. Their presence wasn't universally appreciated. Most of the congregation were, of course, completely ambivalent about those authority figures sitting passively at the back of church. Some would have felt a little bit reassured by a police presence. But there were definitely those who felt uneasy with the 'Old Bill' in the room. 'Why are they here?' 'What do they want?' I remember the time I did a quick straw poll on this very subject, while speaking to a group of fresh, young, middle-class church planters. They all indicated that they would feel safer with the police around.

In fact, Ipsos-MORI's surveys into the most trusted professions have found consistently over 40 years that the majority do trust the police.[1] In its most recent Veracity Survey, conducted in 2020, 71 per cent said that they trust the police to tell the truth.[2] Other authority figures who are well trusted include judges, teachers and doctors. It may be that, just like the room full of young church planters, you too have a high confidence in authority figures, and a police officer walking into church would make you feel safer as well. But if we want to build churches where invisible divides are demolished, it is important to recognize that not everyone has had the same positive experiences of authority figures that we have had. In fact, while someone exerting authority can feel reassuring to some, it can feel intimidating to others. What brings safety to one person can cause another to feel genuinely unsafe.

So why would some people have a negative response to the police? My own experiences of dealings with the police have largely been far from positive: from their attitude and behaviour during my time as a teenager about town and attending football matches up and down the country, to the sarcastic and dismissive responses I've encountered when attending police stations to support some of the young people I know from my community as the official 'appropriate adult'. When my own sons have been robbed of their bikes or phones at knifepoint, the police response has always been a metaphorical shrug of the shoulders and a lame excuse. These experiences, along with many others, have shaped my impression of and attitude towards police authority. My own first-hand experiences have only reinforced a 'them and us' attitude towards those in authority. But for many people that attitude extends far beyond law enforcement.

My local football club, Millwall, has an unofficial slogan: 'No one likes us; we don't care.' As a blog on the *Creative Review* puts it:

During the 70s, Millwall fans earned a reputation for hooliganism. Many at the club felt they were unfairly singled out, particularly as there were plenty of other clubs with hooligan elements in England at the time. Resentment peaked following a 1977 BBC Panorama documentary on Millwall which was criticised for supposedly exaggerating the involvement of the National Front and unfairly demonising the club's supporters. 'No-One Likes Us, We Don't Care' was the fans' defiant response. As Michael Parker, who now runs the NOLU Millwall fanzine (founded by Keith Pegg) says, 'it was us having a pop back at the lazy journalists who published boring negatively biased articles against Millwall'.[3]

It was a community response to a faceless 'them' – in this case journalists and the BBC. It was a defiant chant by a group of people who felt powerless and believed that the press – 'them' – were all against 'us'.

Once an 'us and them' narrative takes hold, it is often reflected in attitudes to authority in general.

In Gillian Evans' book on class and education, she interviews Anita, a working-class woman from Bermondsey:

'It's them and us, that's 'ow it's always been, that's 'ow it'll always be,' Anita laments. 'We are the backbone of the nation and no one gives a f*** about us.' Reacting against dominance, then, working class pride creates the means for dignity; common people fight back defensively with their own values and being common entails, therefore, an inverse snobbery. Posh people are pitied because 'They 'aven't got a clue [about "real" life]'. 'Even with all that education they've got no common sense [no practical skills or understanding about how to deal with common people].' 'They dunno what it means to get by [to know poverty, to struggle against it and survive] and they dunno 'ow to have a good laugh, 'cos of that stiff upper lip.' On the other hand, however, depending on the situation, certain kinds of posh people, like doctors, lawyers and teachers, are respected for their professional expertise. It all depends on the situation whether hatred, pity, resentment, envy or admiration is evinced. Anita is right then about the cultural divide in Britain: each social class is to the other as a people from a distant land with much mutual misunderstanding between the two.[4]

Them and us

We'll look some more at what it means to be 'us' in a moment, but first, what about 'them'? Who are 'they'? 'They' are people in positions of authority. They are the ones who have the power and privilege to make the decisions that affect your life. That could be the national government. Or, in the case of the Millwall fans, the media. 'They' certainly include the police. But 'they' could also be your boss, or someone from the council, like your housing officer or social worker. It could be the disinterested benefit advisor who decides about your Universal Credit.

Magistrates are another obvious one. They are usually drawn from a very different lifestyle and class than those they are sentencing, making decisions about their life and future. As the award-winning, best-selling book *The Secret Barrister* puts it:

> The demographic of most defendants in these courts is homogeneous: society's lost boys and girls, a sorry parade of abused children turned drug abusing adults. Sliding on and off the bottom rung of social function, in and out of homelessness, joblessness and wretched worthlessness, their histories are scabbed with violence, mental ill-health and chaos, and their present lies in a parallel universe where the middle-class ambition of the Good Life is replaced with a desperate scrapping for daily survival.[5]

After that bleak description of defendants in the court, the author turns his attention to the magistrates themselves:

> It takes a certain type of character to volunteer to sit in judgement over one's fellow citizens as a hobby. And it so happens, that to the present day, that type of character has been white, middle aged and middle class, with a traditional conservative leaning.[6]

What's described here is a huge cultural disconnect that is based on class and power. Working-class people can often feel powerless when interacting with authority figures, whoever they are, and that feeling of impotence can lead to huge frustrations. Whether it's the police, a magistrate, someone from the council who you feel is tying you up with their red tape, or the officious senior manager at the kids' school using unnecessarily baffling, class-rooted vocabulary (what I mean by that is deliberately using long words and jargon to emphasize position and authority). But here's the thing: people may feel frustrated, but they're not all passive, and they will react. When you feel patronized or threatened, you can either surrender to the other person's position and power or you can push back and fight. And when that happens, lots of people don't like it.

We saw in the previous chapter that there is still a strong sense of group identity in a lot of working-class communities, a sense of being part of something bigger. One of the ways in which this expresses itself is in the Trade Union movement.

Workers' rights

I (Paul) sometimes ask myself: why is it that, even though Christians were so influential through the history of the trade union movement, today the vast majority of Christians I meet are generally opposed to the work of trade unions? Lots of people have an almost dispensationalist view: 'We needed unions back then but things are different now.' One church leader I spoke to commented, 'Back then the unions fought because of need; now they fight because of their greed.' The irony of that comment was the fact that his experience was in the healthcare sector, where the majority of employees are in low-paid jobs.

As I explored the differing sympathies shown towards trade unions, I spent some time with a Communications Workers Union (CWU) representative, Roy. I was keen to find out how Roy reconciled his role as a union representative with his Christian faith. He said, 'If you saw somebody lying injured in the road, you'd go and help them. If you was at work and saw someone getting bullied you're going to help them too, what's the difference? And if the bullies are the employers, then so be it.'

Roy is genuinely surprised that people struggle to understand that he can be a trade unionist and a Christian: 'I can't see the difference in wanting to protect people and ensure they don't live in poverty. Please don't tell me that as a trade unionist I haven't got the right to stand up for other people, 'cos I have. I'm surprised a lot of people don't see that I'm fighting for justice.'

One church leader spoke to him, laughing, 'I see your boys are out on strike again.'

Roy answered, 'So you think that's amusing that people are losing money, do you?' He walked away.

He explains, 'I know I joke a lot, but representing people is a serious issue; defending people's rights is a serious issue. And when Christians make stupid remarks like [the unions] are a tool of the devil and all that nonsense, they're talking out of complete ignorance.'

Roy isn't exaggerating – he literally heard a church leader say in front of thousands of people that unions are an instrument of the devil. To someone who is heavily invested in this as a justice issue, comments like that hurt. Roy says, 'I expect more of Christians, I suppose. I expect Christians to be more sympathetic towards people's needs and I expect them to at least attempt to understand when we withdraw our labour that it's a last resort by people on low wages, in order to improve their lot. To say to someone who earns 400 quid a week, "give up £100 of that this week [to go on strike] and probably for the next few weeks," it's a massive thing.'

When it comes to the issue of authority, it can be a difficult line for Christians to walk. The Bible is clear that we should submit to authority, but also that we should be actively pursuing justice.

To do that, we need to hold in tension that some authority is good, and some authority is bad, but no authority is given by anyone other than God. We need to take seriously the complaints of the powerless and be a voice for the voiceless (see Prov. 31.8-9), which sometimes means standing against powerful people and systems that either deliberately or inadvertently oppress people. At the same time, we need to honour those in authority and seek peace in our communities. The church actually has a vital role to play here in bridging divisions.

As Gillan Scott puts it on the God & Politics blog:

Christians have to live with an apparent paradox. We're called to fight injustice. God has many serious words to say against those who oppress their workers and treat them badly. However on several occasions in the New Testament we are told to submit to authorities over us. 1 Peter 2:18 says, '*Slaves, in reverent fear of God submit yourselves to your masters, not only to those who are good and considerate, but also to those who are harsh.*' In Romans 13:1, Paul writes, '*Let everyone be subject to the governing authorities, for there is no authority except that which God has established.*' These verses need to be read carefully in context, but the underlying message is that Christians need to try and establish a balance between knowing when to act against genuine injustice and when to submit to authority in a gracious and unselfish way. Both of these courses of action can potentially be costly and at the times when we have to make these judgement calls, we really need to be asking for God's wisdom.[7]

One of the challenges in church life is that we do believe in God-ordained authority, but it must look very different from authority in the world – especially when there are so many abuses of it by powerful people. We need to intentionally model humble, servant leadership. Jesus is Lord of all, yet 'came not to be served but to serve' (Matt. 20.28 ESV UK), and famously even washed his disciples' feet. He demonstrated it with his actions – his whole life was given to serving others – but he was also clear with those who would become his apostles about the leadership style he desires:

> You know that the rulers of the Gentiles lord it over them, and their high officials exercise authority over them. Not so with you. Instead, whoever wants to become great among you must be your servant, and whoever wants to be first must be your slave.
> (Matt. 20.25–27)

Those of us in authority need to serve as Jesus served, not lording it over people, not clinging to power, but empowering others. Those of us under authority need to submit to godly authority and stand up for any who are oppressed by ungodly authority. We respect and honour authority figures, while fighting for justice. The two are not mutually exclusive, but it can be a hard balance to get right. This comes down not just to how we act, but also to how we speak.

Earning trust

One way to begin to explore how different people in your community feel about authority is to ask the following questions:

- Who makes the decisions that affect the quality of life in my community?
- How are those decisions taken?
- Who decides what type of housing should be built or demolished?

It's often the case that decision-makers don't live 'round here'; they're usually not part of the community, with the shared interests and experiences we looked at in the previous chapter. If the authorities are generally not trusted by the working-class people around us, as churches we need to be very aware of that. And we also need to take a good look at ourselves and ask, 'Are we seen to be part of "them", the authority figures who aren't to be trusted, or part of "us" – a welcoming community where all are accepted?'

If we want to be effective in reaching into working-class communities, we, as Christians, need to work hard to earn the trust of those communities. I (Paul) believe it's to our advantage as the church that we're not seen as part of 'them' – without being disrespectful to authority, we need to show that we're not the same as 'them', by which I mean we are not giving preferential treatment to the powerful. If the church is seen as the opposition, as 'them', it's likely we won't be trusted.

Ultimately, the church should not be 'us' or 'them' – we want to break down the barriers between the powerful and the powerless. One of the most moving demonstrations of the gospel's effectiveness to break down invisible divides I (Natalie) have seen is when a convicted burglar who had been in and out of prison was baptized at the same time as one of the police officers who had previously arrested him. Both had recently encountered Jesus and become Christians. Before, they had been 'enemies'; now they were brothers in Christ, cheering each other on as they were, one after the other, fully immersed in the baptism pool. This is what should happen time and time again in church life – 'us' and 'them' side by side, worshipping together, breaking bread together, sharing our lives with each other.

9

Motivations

I (Natalie) have a friend who would describe herself as upper class. She is very wealthy (and incredibly generous). When we talk about our childhoods, schools and teenage years, we have very little in common. A typical studio flat near her central London, three-storey house goes on the market for almost four times as much as my two-bedroom flat in a deprived part of the south coast.

When we spend time together, it is easy to spot the differences between us. The things that could divide us are not invisible, for the most part, whereas the things we have in common are harder to see, but are still there. Through talking to this friend, I have discovered that in some aspects of life, the working classes have more in common with the upper classes than with the middle classes. Of course, like much of what we are exploring in this book, the following are generalizations. But in talking about my up-bringing and hers, we have discovered that among our peers there is a shared hatred of camping, an equal commitment to wearing clothes until they are literally falling apart, and even some words that sound similar in my common voice and her upper-class accent (for example, 'shower' – we both miss out the w and say it as if it only has one syllable, but my friend's version sounds posher than mine!).

Some of these differences and similarities are amusing. Nevertheless, it is important for anyone wishing to overcome invisible divides between the classes to reflect on the motivations that underpin our behaviours and attitudes.

Hidden factors

In her seminal work *A Framework for Understanding Poverty*, Dr Ruby K. Payne explored some of the hidden factors behind the ways those in poverty, the middle classes and the wealthy in the USA think about money, clothing, time, family and so on. Some of Dr Payne's conclusions map just as easily over a UK context of working-, middle- and upper-class structures.[1]

For example, the most common question working-class parents will ask their children at meal times is, 'Have you had enough?' Quantity is the most important thing. One of my friends from a local estate puts it like this about dinners for her kids: 'All I care about is if their stomachs are full.' With the middle classes, the question is more likely to be, 'Do you like it?' Quality is important. 'I want my children to try different foods and experience different tastes,' says one of my middle-class friends.

These are generalizations again, of course, but it can be really helpful to consider differences like these in church contexts. Over the years, I have learnt to ask questions at meal tables, and a year spent working in China taught me to try unfamiliar foods – it broadened my food horizon substantially. Yet I have lost count of how many times I have felt awkward at meal tables because of not knowing what is in front of me. In a work context, I have had to seek help from friends or colleagues in restaurants where I don't recognize items on the menu, but far more often I have had to ask in someone's home what it is that they have placed in front of me.

This is not necessarily a big deal, but it can be an invisible divide that leads to uncomfortable social encounters. More important than any awkwardness – disclosed or hidden – is the power balance. It can foster a sense of inequality and create a dynamic where one party feels inferior. In my experience, this is particularly evidenced by a lack of reciprocity. There are very few people in church life that I would feel comfortable about welcoming to my home for a meal, and on the rare occasions when I do invite people from different backgrounds from mine, I seek extensive advice from friends about how to make a good impression, what to cook, how to serve up food, table presentation and so on.

Half-empty bags of crisps

Relatedly, these differences can manifest in church life too – through small groups and on Sundays. I once hosted a small group at my flat and, because I feel out of depth in such situations (even after 25 years as a Christian), I asked everyone to bring snacks and drinks. I bought some myself, but I would have been mortified if I had got the quantity wrong. One of my friends arrived with two big bags of crisps that were half full. A couple of light-hearted comments were made, just jokes, but it struck me at the time: why isn't that absolutely fine? Surely it should be OK to bring what you have, rather than having to buy something specific?

Martin Charlesworth and I wrote in *A Church for the Poor*:

if it's common for people in your group to bring expensive bottles of drink to social gatherings, someone with less disposable income may feel pressure to try to fit in, or they may feel excluded from the group as a result of not being able to afford the same as everyone else.[2]

A specific example given by the editor of that book was small groups where typically people would bring pricey bottles of smoothies, and she was not sure how it would be perceived if someone were to turn up with a supermarket value brand of lemonade, for example.

Even the coffee we serve on Sundays can be divisive. Some churches go down the route of wanting the very best filter coffee, as a symbol of the value they place on people who attend or visit them on Sundays. Others take the opposite approach, wanting to ensure the coffee they serve will be familiar and affordable to all who come. Neither is right or wrong, but it is dismissive of the invisible divides that can make a huge difference to someone's experience of church if we don't consider how our decisions might affect people from different walks of life.

Beyond food and drink motivations linked to quality versus quantity, Dr Payne highlights other areas of difference in the USA that are also relevant in the UK. She points out, for example, that even the way we think about personality can be differently motivated. She suggests that, for the working classes or those in poverty, it has more to do with entertainment. This means that a sense of humour is important, along with an ability to laugh at oneself and not take oneself too seriously. But for the middle classes, she suggests that achievement is highly valued because personality is about acquisition and stability. For the upper classes (or in Dr Payne's framework, the wealthy), personality is all about connections, because it is financial, political and social connections that are most valued.

Dr Payne's framework makes the case for differences between classes across possessions, money, social emphasis, clothing, personality, food, money, time, education, destiny, language, family structure, worldview, love, driving forces and humour.

What drives us

One of the most interesting distinctions she makes is her proposition that the working classes are driven primarily by survival, relationships and entertainment, while the middle classes are predominantly driven by work and achievement. Of course, this will vary from person to person according to temperament, experiences and a range of other factors, but in my experience there is more than a semblance of truth in Dr Payne's assertion here.

These motivating factors affect how we view every aspect of life. Consider for yourself: do you think of work as a means to an end, or as something that gives you purpose? This is something that has changed for me over many years of being surrounded by middle-class Christians. As I have myself become more middle class (though mostly outwardly), I have noticed that I have increasingly seen work as something I am 'called to', something that gives me a sense of significance and purpose, something in which I can very easily start to find my identity. But that was not always the case.

I notice it in myself most starkly in conversations I have with my mum. Over the last few years, I have been increasingly baffled by her responses to my achievements and opportunities at work. When I told her I had been invited to be a keynote speaker at a national Christian conference, she said, 'You should say no. You're too busy.' When I told her I had the opportunity to write another book, she said, 'Do you really want to do that? It can be quite stressful for you.' When I told her I had been offered the role of Chief Executive at the national Christian charity Jubilee+, she said, 'Are you sure you want to do that?' Later, when I was experiencing self-doubt and imposter syndrome around taking on such a significant role, she said, 'Well, don't worry. Just give it a go. If you're no good at it, you can quit.' (Everyone else I expressed self-doubt to encouraged me that I could do it, or learn to do it.)

My mum is not being unkind or critical, or lacking belief in me. As I have pondered many months over what is going on with these unusual responses to the things opening up for me in my work, I realized that it is simply that my motivations have changed hugely. My mum worked faithfully in one organization for 28 years. She didn't seek more responsibility. In fact, when she was encouraged to progress into a managerial role, she could not understand why she would even contemplate it. She was not bothered about promotions. She was concerned with paying the bills, and that was that – well, maybe with having good friendships at her workplace too. Her job was first and foremost about earning money to live; second, it was about relationships. A sense of purpose or fulfilment was not really a factor at all.

So just as I have been baffled by my mum's responses to the opportunities I have had, so has she been baffled about why I would take on greater responsibilities when I am already busy, I already sometimes find work stressful, I already find myself working outside traditional hours, and so on. My mum's decisions, especially about work, have been based much more on survival and relationships, whereas mine have increasingly become about achievement and satisfaction.

Survival or purpose?

Just as the differences in motivations when it comes to food and drink play out in our individual lives and in church life, the same is true of working to pay the bills compared with working for a sense of achievement or purpose.

Many preachers emphasize that work existed prior to the Fall. God created us to work. It is not a result of sin. It is something we were made to do. It gives us dignity and stability. Work as a general concept is part of our purpose, but in the western, middle-class world, for many this has been stretched to make specific work *the* purpose of our lives. It has become central, rather than just being a part of how we were made and what we were made to do. This can lead to confusing conversations within church settings, where some might be perceived to have a lack of ambition while others are seen to be overly ambitious. This might be true, of course, but sometimes it is just a misunderstanding about how we are wired by our upbringing.

While the Bible makes it clear that work is important for all, it doesn't speak much about the value we should place on career. If we understand this, we can start to see how we might be imposing middle-class values on church teaching and activities when we talk about things like purpose, satisfaction and achievement through our jobs. To give a couple of examples of how this can put up invisible divides, I have heard many people in church life make dismissive comments or quips about 'working in McDonald's'. When speaking on faith and work, a preacher Paul was listening to dismissed road-sweeping as a better-than-nothing job, but he wouldn't want his son to do it. When such statements come out of our mouths, even if they are light-hearted or flippant, they reveal an attitude in our hearts. Namely, that working in a fast-food restaurant or sweeping the roads is not as good as other jobs.

When that happens, we need to challenge ourselves about our ways of thinking. Why do we think some jobs are better than others? Is it based on pay? There is nothing in the Bible to suggest a hierarchy of jobs. Work gives us dignity because it is predominantly about provision and supporting ourselves, not acquisition or achievement. Of course, there are many people in the Bible who had significant roles, wealth and status – for example, King David. But he started out as a shepherd. Many of those raised to prominence – to 'career highs', so to speak – knew times of humility first. And for those who didn't . . . so often we see things going horribly awry for those who had no experience of humble beginnings.

Jesus was a carpenter. Peter was a fisherman. Paul was a tent-maker. Yet manual labourers are conspicuously absent from our mostly middle-class churches. Might this be, in part, because of our different attitudes to types of work, and what work is supposed to be about? We shouldn't be surprised when some people are perfectly content with lives that we can't relate to. Before Paul (my co-author, not the apostle!) became a Christian, he had achieved all of his life's ambitions – he had a home (rented), a job as a bricklayer and family (girlfriend and baby). He was happy and content, and why shouldn't he have been?

Hopefully, it goes without saying that there is a place for speaking about personal fulfilment. But biblically speaking, this is to be found in the Great Commandments and the Great Commission: we are to love God, to love our neighbours as ourselves and to make disciples. Where we work is not as important as the relationships we build. Loving well is the ultimate goal of the Christian faith – becoming more Christlike by loving God and loving others – and therefore this is where we find our ultimate sense of purpose.

Whether or not we can clearly see differences in our motivations, it is at least worth spending some time considering how different groups of people think about different aspects of life, from food to work, as we have explored. The reason it is a good use of our time is because if we fail to understand the hidden habits and motivations of a group, we will not see the invisible divides that might be excluding, alienating or 'othering' those we would like to have fully involved in church life, and indeed in our own lives.

10

Aspirations

One of the first things that changed for me when I (Natalie) became a Christian was my aspirations – my hopes and expectations for the future. It was not that I hadn't aspired to anything before, but when I look back now, I realize that as a child and teenager, I just assumed my life would pan out a certain way.

There wasn't a range of options set out before me.

I didn't even think about aspirations. If anyone had told me back then that I would one day become the chief executive of a national charity, it would have baffled me. It isn't simply that it would have seemed unattainable for someone like me. More than that: I wouldn't have understood why that was something to aim for. Growing up in relative poverty, a job like that wasn't even on my radar.

I did want to write books. I imagined I would write cheap, cheesy romance novels. In fact, when I was 11 years old, I wrote to Mills & Boon to ask how I could write for them when I was older. So a lack of aspirations isn't necessarily about a lack of dreams. It has more to do with a lack of opportunities, leading to an inability to imagine that life can look significantly different from what you already know.

When I started following Jesus, there was a popular Christian band called Delirious? who released a song called 'History makers'. Though I have since come to find some of the lyrics unhelpful, back then – as a newly converted teenager – the idea that I could actually make history contributed to an awakened sense that my life might be about more than finding a way to pay the bills and hoping that way would make me happy.

Before becoming a Christian, I had never contemplated that my life might make a difference, or even that it might have an influence on people around me. The idea that I have been created to have an impact, even a small one, was completely new to me. So was the concept of my life being about more than just me and my immediate loved ones.

It isn't just that I didn't think about the bigger picture. For me there was no bigger picture. My world view and my choices seemed very narrow, but I didn't feel perturbed by this. It wasn't something I pondered at all.

God's big vision

One of the Bible passages that is so precious to me now is Isaiah 61, because it speaks of God's big vision for people like me, with backgrounds similar to mine, and much tougher. So often, only the first couple of verses are quoted and preached about:

> The Spirit of the Lord GOD is upon me,
> because the LORD has anointed me
> to bring good news to the poor;
> he has sent me to bind up the broken-hearted,
> to proclaim liberty to the captives,
> and the opening of the prison to those who are bound;
> to proclaim the year of the LORD's favour,
> and the day of vengeance of our God;
> to comfort all who mourn; to grant to those who mourn in Zion –
> to give them a beautiful headdress instead of ashes,
> the oil of gladness instead of mourning,
> and the garment of praise instead of a faint spirit . . .
> (Isa. 61.1–3 ESV UK)

But for me, it is the rest of verse 3 and then verse 4 that have helped me to see that God's vision for my life is for it to be about more than just myself:

. . . that they may be called oaks of righteousness,
the planting of the LORD, that he may be glorified.
They shall build up the ancient ruins;
they shall raise up the former devastations;
they shall repair the ruined cities,
the devastations of many generations.
(Isa. 61.3–4 ESV UK)

After becoming a Christian, the first significantly noticeable change in my thinking was to do with my perspective about my life and my place in the world. My horizons broadened; the path in front of me suddenly seemed to have options, and to be wider than I had imagined. I realized, for the first time, that whatever God was doing in my own heart and life was not just for me, but for those I came into contact with too.

On a trip to Kenya in 2016, I noticed a similar perspective at work in the lives of young people supported by the charity Compassion.[1] Its sponsorship programme provides education, medical care and food. While in Nairobi, I heard the stories of several 20-something Compassion 'graduates'. As they talked about the difference sponsorship had made to their childhoods and to their families, as well as what they were currently doing, they all expressed a deep sense of responsibility to their community. In many ways, Compassion had liberated them from the slums into which they were born, but none of them saw it this way. They all talked about getting qualified – as nurses or lawyers or teachers or doctors – *so that* they could take the opportunity they had been given and use it for the good of others who were just like them.

This is the wonderful heart of God for people who have less. We see it outlined beautifully in the Isaiah 61 passage above, where it is not the rich and powerful who renew, rebuild and restore, but those who have struggled and suffered. They – those who have been poor, broken-hearted, captives, bound, mourning – become the very people who rebuild ancient ruins, raise up devastated places and repair ruined communities.

'Hell-on-sea'

Hastings, where I grew up and now live again, was once called 'Hell-on-sea' by a national newspaper. But that's not how God sees it. For all of its deprivation – for all of the statistic tables it tops to do with low educational attainment, ill-health, substance misuse, mental health issues, poor-quality housing and so on – God does not write it off, but he has a plan to raise up people like me (and people with much harder backgrounds than mine) to make a difference, to be an integral part of its renewal and restoration, to speak a better word over the community.

But often in society, and sadly in church life too, we look to the powerful, the well educated and the affluent as those we consider to have the most potential for leadership and impact.

That might be because children with my kind of background and worse are 'less likely to do well at school, less likely to have aspirations for the future, less likely to be healthy and more likely to die prematurely, less likely to have a well-paid job when they are adults'.[2] Research by the Child Poverty Action Group (CPAG) shows that family income has a significant impact across all areas of children's lives – affecting them not just materially, but also relationally, emotionally, mentally, intellectually and physically.[3]

It is absolutely true that in the kingdom of God, statistics like these can be completely turned around – but there is a degree to which people from certain backgrounds might be inhibited from aspiring and flourishing in church life if they are not nurtured in a helpful way (at best) or if they are disqualified on the basis of not fitting in with the traditional mould we think of when we think about potential leaders or even 'pillars of the church' (at worst). Interestingly, neither Paul nor I aspired to church leadership roles, though we both have them now. We were both content with our secular jobs. There can be a misguided belief among 'high achievers' that the thing to aspire to in church is a leadership role.

The fact is, biblically speaking, we all have something to contribute and something to learn from each other, irrespective of background. But some may discount themselves or not even be considered by those in leadership over them because of their background – unwittingly, of course, but the result is the same.

All made in his image

The truth is that everyone we have been placed alongside in our lives is actually God's gift to us, in one way or another. We are meant to leave a trace on the lives of those we spend time with, and they are meant to influence and have an impact on us too. American church leader, speaker and author Tim Keller states it plainly: 'God doesn't make junk.'[4] Each one of us is made in the image of God, which means that each one of us carries some aspect of God's divine imprint – we carry something of Almighty God within us that reflects him to those around us. John Piper puts it like this: 'God created us in his image so that we would display or reflect or communicate who he is, how great he is, and what he is like.'[5]

One of the biggest struggles of my Christian faith has been coming to truly believe that I have worth, that I have value, no matter what my background or how other people might perceive me or treat me, or even what they speak over me. The truth is that my upbringing, my life experiences and other people's perceptions of me and limits on me do not speak the loudest word over me. God does. And he says that I am becoming an oak of righteousness, for the display of his splendour and for the rebuilding of broken people and places around me.

This is true for all of us. Every single one of us matters. Our worth isn't dependent on our status or achievements, our education or talent or wealth or friendship group. It is wholly dependent upon being made in the image of God, and reflecting something of who he is to those around us. British writer and theologian G. K. Chesterton wrote, 'You matter. I matter. It's the hardest thing in theology to believe.'[6]

But it is not just difficult to believe it for ourselves. In a culture where success and status are idolized, it can be hard for us to believe that others matter too. Of course, we may not say this, or even think it overtly, but it can so often, so easily, be demonstrated by our actions and our assumptions about the people around us.

The reason we need to cross invisible divides when it comes to aspirations and valuing people is because God wants his church to represent him fully, meaning we need diversity. We need each person to bring his or her unique, image-bearing self to be built together into the body of Christ with all of the other unique, image-bearing trophies of grace.

Locard's Principle

I used to work for the Safer Hastings Partnership, which brought together a group of statutory agencies to tackle crime in my town. Forensic science plays a crucial role in solving crimes, and one of the pioneering ideas in the development of forensic science was presented by Dr Edmond Locard, who is sometimes called 'the French Sherlock Holmes'.

Locard formulated one of the most influential ideas in forensic science, which is essentially that if I burgle your home, I will leave traces of myself in your home and will carry traces of your home away with me. Locard's Principle is that I cannot commit a crime without leaving traces of my presence. It may sound obvious to us today, but Locard's Principle that 'every contact leaves a trace' was groundbreaking.

It holds truth that is even more powerful for us as Christians than it is in the criminal justice world. Every contact leaves a trace. We are meant to have an impact on each other. It's why there are so many 'one another' references in the New Testament letters. How I act affects you, and vice versa. This is how it is meant to be in the kingdom of God. We need each other. We were made for community. We were created and called to be the bride of Christ, together, collectively, irrespective of our differences. Not despite them, but because of them.

We became much more aware of the idea that 'every contact leaves a trace' during the coronavirus pandemic. To protect each other, we wore face masks, sanitized our hands repeatedly, went into lockdown, stayed two metres apart from each other and so on. All of this was to stop us from passing on the virus, which spread incredibly easily. During the pandemic, we became aware like never in our lifetime before that every contact has the potential to leave a trace – in this case, a deadly one.

God's plan for us – no matter what our backgrounds or experiences – is that we will leave a trace of him on everyone we encounter. That will look different for each of us. It is supposed to. Each one of us is unique, and God has intentionally placed us alongside specific people in our families, friendship groups, neighbourhoods, communities and churches. We can and should leave a positive trace on those around us, both within the church and outside.

He has placed each one of us specifically – with our unique mix of personality, temperament, life story, experiences, battles we've been through – in the lives of others, deliberately, so that we can leave a trace of him with them. This means that every relationship is two-way, and no one can be written off.

Indispensable and honoured

In the kingdom of God, it is not about survival of the fittest, but about us all being built together to strengthen one another. We do this as iron sharpening iron, but also by bearing with one another in love and patience and forgiveness. In fact, biblically speaking, we should esteem those whom the world would discard or discount. As it says in 1 Corinthians 1.27–31:

> But God chose what is foolish in the world to shame the wise; God chose what is weak in the world to shame the strong; God chose what is low and despised in the world, even things that are not, to bring to nothing the things that are, so that no human being might boast in the presence of God. And because of him you are in Christ Jesus, who became to us wisdom from God, righteousness and sanctification and redemption, so that, as it is written, 'Let the one who boasts, boast in the Lord.'
> (ESV UK)

This should challenge our attitudes about both ourselves and other people. God chooses the foolish and weak intentionally. That is his plan, and it should affect our attitudes towards people, as we see further on in 1 Corinthians 12.12–27:

> For just as the body is one and has many members, and all the members of the body, though many, are one body, so it is with Christ. For in one Spirit we were all baptized into one body – Jews or Greeks, slaves or free – and all were made to drink of one Spirit.
> For the body does not consist of one member but of many . . . If the whole body were an eye, where would be the sense of hearing? If the whole body were an ear, where would be the sense of smell? *But as it is, God arranged the members in the body, each one of them, as he chose . . .*
> *. . . the parts of the body that seem to be weaker are indispensable, and on those parts of the body that we think less*

honourable we bestow the greater honour, and our unpresent-able parts are treated with greater modesty, which our more presentable parts do not require. *But God has so composed the body, giving greater honour to the part that lacked it, that there may be no division in the body, but that the members may have the same care for one another.* If one member suffers, all suffer together; if one member is honoured, all rejoice together.

Now you are the body of Christ and individually members of it.

(ESV UK, emphasis added)

If we take these verses to heart, ponder them deeply and let them shape us, they will displace any arrogance, any superiority, any sense of one-way discipleship. If every disciple of Jesus were to live like this, then we would know we all have something to learn from each other. The invisible divides of class would disappear as we all – working classes, middle classes and upper classes – sought to lay down our preferences, our ways of doing things, and humbly reflect God to each other and learn about his character and deeds from each other. That is how we all mature into oaks of righteousness, for his glory and for the good of everyone around us.

Everyone you meet is made in the image of God: the family member who most annoys you, the colleague who rubs you up the wrong way, the person in your church small group whom you simply cannot relate to at all. Everyone who comes alongside you can uniquely reflect something of God to you, if you let them.

Tim Keller puts the challenge like this:

Every person that comes across your path, you need to treat with a sacredness, a reverence, a respect, a concern for their individuality, a kindness, never writing people off . . . We must treat everyone with grace, everyone with gentleness . . . Do you?[7]

Let's stretch it one step further, though, for the purposes of this chapter and this book. Do you treat everyone as valuable and having a valuable contribution to bring to church life, and to your life? God challenged me personally on this a few years ago – and the challenge is ongoing – when he pointed out to me that if I cannot see the image of God in someone, the problem isn't with them. It's with me.

Part 3

CHURCH LIFE

11

Diverse, not divided

I (Natalie) am really blessed to have close friends from wildly differing backgrounds and life experiences. One of my friends lives in a very large house in the middle of nowhere and does not have to think before spending money, whether on something large or small. Another of my good friends, when asked if she wants to do something socially, frequently replies that she cannot really afford to go out so suggests we meet up in her home. I have friends who go from week to week not knowing if they will have enough money for food, and a couple of others who are millionaires. Sometimes there are misunderstandings and even disagreements arising from our differences, but my life and my faith are enriched by having a circle of friends who are not all the same. If we are willing to ask questions and hear honest answers, so we can get to know how the other person thinks, there is no need for anything that could divide us – invisible or plain to see – to be insurmountable.

This is definitely the case for Christians. God doesn't call us to something we cannot do, so if he has called us to tear down dividing walls of hostility and to be in his family together, then we can do that. It involves effort and energy. It is hard work, seeking to understand people who think differently from the way we do and who are coming from an entirely different starting place, but it is not impossible. We start by seeing each person as someone loved by God and made in his image, and then we build upon that by recognizing that Jesus calls people from all walks of life to follow him and be part of his church. We are being built together, which isn't always comfortable, but it is the way God has made it to be. We honour him when we honour one another. We glorify him when we cross invisible divides and allow ourselves to learn from those around us, as iron sharpens iron (Prov. 27.17), so that we might all be conformed to the image of Christ (Rom. 8.29), one degree of glory at a time (1 Cor. 3.18 ESV UK).

The previous section highlighted a number of areas of life in which the working classes tend to think or act differently from the middle classes. Neither is necessarily wrong or right – each group has much to learn from the other – but we have deliberately challenged the middle classes more than the working classes because the former make up the dominant culture in our churches, and the onus has to be on the majority to make space for those who are in the minority. However, no group has the monopoly on life skills or correct attitudes or healthy behaviour. Each of us needs to walk in humility alongside our brothers and sisters in Christ and the people outside the church we are seeking to support or welcome into our church communities.

This is a challenge for us all. Most of us inherently believe that our ways of thinking and doing things are 'right', otherwise we would change them. Submitting ourselves to the preferences of others, examining ourselves soberly and making changes for the good of others – these are all important aspects of Christian maturity, for disciples from all backgrounds.

The purpose of highlighting our differences is not to entrench them, but to reveal them so that we can move towards each other. If we don't understand that someone else's experience of money or community or authority or faith might be very different from ours, it won't take long before we accidentally alienate or even clash with those around us. By shining a light on some key areas of difference, our aim has been to equip majority-middle-class churches (leaders and members) to see blind spots and possibly even prejudices that might be making others feel that they don't fit in. This is the first step in understanding some of these different ways of thinking and acting, so that we can be active in demonstrating greater acceptance and valuing of people who are looking in on or who are part of our churches, but who are not included in, or comfortable with, the dominant culture.

Normal middle-class behaviour is not the same as Christian behaviour. Neither is typical working-class behaviour the same as Christian behaviour. Jesus transcends all divisions, calling us to something far more radical. We need to be able to decipher between the norms of the dominant culture and what is actually biblical, Christlike behaviour, so that we don't push people in our churches to conform to the standards of the majority, but rather only to what we see in Jesus. Taking the time to think these things through, then to change any of our attitudes that we recognize need to change, will create a more accessible culture in our churches.

We know that many of you will have picked up this book because your story mirrors mine and Paul's and, like us, you might be longing for churches where more people 'like you' can find a place without merging into the dominant culture around you. We imagine many of you reading, especially if you live in a deprived area or if you're involved in mercy ministries or social action, will have already recognized a disconnect between your projects and your church activities, and between the people you meet in one compared with those you meet in the other. We are sure that some of you reading are church leaders who have already become aware that your congregation's demographic doesn't match that of the surrounding community.

Whatever drew you to this book, reading about some of the significant invisible divides between the classes has hopefully been helpful to you. Quite possibly it has felt uncomfortable at times – we have sought to provoke. But raising awareness of the differences between us is only the start. In this short final section, we offer some thoughts on what it might look like practically to make space for those who are from a working-class background and currently missing from many of our churches across the UK. Largely this is to do with our culture of leadership and our structure and style of meetings – these have a big impact and will be significant factors behind the lack of working-class people in our churches. We hope this will be of practical help so that people from all walks of life will know they are included and valued in our churches, without having to modify their behaviour and attitudes to match those around them, and can just be like Jesus.

12

Meetings

During the coronavirus pandemic in 2020 and 2021, I (Natalie) found church meetings hard. I'm single and live on my own, so there were points during online, live-streamed meetings where I felt I couldn't engage, such as breaking bread. I had no one to break it with. Then, when we could meet in person again, church meetings highlighted my 'aloneness'. Though I was in a lovely 'bubble' with friends and their two small children, they didn't return to church meetings in person at first because there were no activities for their children, and then later, when they did come back, they were usually busy serving on various teams. This meant that if I went to a church meeting, owing to social distancing rules I had to sit on my own.

I remember walking into one meeting where I had hoped a friend in my bubble had saved me a seat, but she hadn't had a chance to even get herself one, so I stood around, feeling lost. Someone invited me to sit with them, but the lockdown rules meant I wasn't allowed.

For these reasons, meetings highlighted my difference from the majority, my 'otherness', and that reminded me of my early experiences of church life.

Bewildered

The first time I ever walked into a meeting at the church where I later became a Christian, I found it a bewildering experience. Nothing was as I expected. First of all, they didn't meet in a church building, but in a school hall. Second, I noticed that they had a band, with a drummer, guitarist, bassist and so on. That was a surprise. Third,

125

there were young people there – teenagers my age who looked as if they actually wanted to be there.

There were plenty of culture shocks for me about church meetings, with many of them just coming down to familiarity, or lack of it. But how we carry out our meetings can put up invisible divides between certain groups of people – usually completely inadvertently, which is why in this chapter we want to put forward some thoughts for reflection. This is not to say that all of these aspects of church life should be changed to suit one group over another, just that if we don't think about how they might be creating barriers, then we won't be able to help some of the people we would love to attract to church feel at ease when they come.

Every element of our church meetings will suit some people and not others. For example, as mentioned earlier, the coffee served can be a point of contention in many churches. Some opt for the finest filter coffee, wanting to give people the very best as a way to communicate that they are valued. Perhaps it is also to demonstrate that church is not second-rate to the world around us, but can model excellence. I have heard that argued. However, there will be some people who come to our churches who have never tried filter coffee and find it off-putting, maybe even pretentious or extravagant. There is no right or wrong when it comes to which coffee to serve (though I know some would argue with me on this!), but the point is to think through whether or not we are offering what the majority of people in society might be most familiar with. By asking this, we at least take the time to explore the thinking behind our choices and to analyse whether we have made the best decision.

Content and context

More important than coffee, though, is to think through each of the elements of our actual meetings themselves. This would include how long the sermon should be, bearing in mind that most people only ever find themselves sitting still and listening to someone talk for 40 minutes in a classroom or university lecture theatre. If you are a thoroughly engaging speaker who has mastered the art of holding people's attention, you can get away with it. (But you might not be the best judge of this!)

It's not just about length, but it's also about content. If all of your anecdotes are about playing golf or cricket, for example, these will be hard for some people in your congregation to relate to (in general, not just when it comes to class). Something that might be very normal in your life – such as lending your lawnmower to your neighbours – might be a million miles away from the lives of those you're speaking to, who may live in flats and not have access to a garden.

The way we speak about issues in society needs to take into account the different ways people experience those issues. If we speak on hot topics such as immigration (which affects working-class communities very differently from the way it affects comfortable middle-class communities) or climate change (which might not be such a pressing concern for someone struggling to feed their children), it is obviously vital to do so biblically, but we need to help people from all walks of life know how to apply this in their contexts. If any social issue shone a spotlight on the lack of understanding between different classes, it was the Brexit referendum. I (Natalie) spoke with a business owner in his early thirties during the debate on our place in the European Union, and he said that he felt completely alienated in church now because he planned to vote leave. He found that every time Brexit was mentioned – whether during meetings or over coffee – it was assumed that the 'right' Christian way to vote was to remain in the EU, which left him feeling misunderstood, ostracized and offended.

Likewise, as we saw earlier, if you denigrate certain groups of people when you preach – whether it's readers of *The Sun* newspaper, or road-sweepers – then you are obviously going to alienate anyone who identifies with that.

Beyond your own stories and examples, though, there is the question of *how* you communicate: is your sermon like a university lecture, or have you honed the skill of storytelling so that you can have a broader appeal? Have you thought about how different groups of people learn or take in information?

Another point on the subject of sermon content is how we factor in teaching on some of the invisible divides between us. If we want to have truly diverse churches where people from all walks of life feel equally welcomed, accepted and valued, then we need to teach on it, because embracing difference does not come naturally to most of us. If we don't have a place for teaching on how people from different backgrounds experience and approach some of the things we looked at in Part 2 of this book – such as communication, community and authority – then we are likely to misunderstand each other (at best), find ourselves offended by each other or (at worst) feel that we cannot be in church community with the people around us. This might not need to be a Sunday sermon series (though it could be), but could be drip-fed into several sermons in the same way we frequently talk about prayer, Bible reading, etc., without necessarily dedicating whole talks to them every month or two. Equally, it might be part of a 'joining course' or 'membership course', if you have such a thing at your church, or perhaps reflected in the online content you put out through your website, app, YouTube channel or social media. The key question is not whether or not it is important to speak about differences, but how we will do so in a way that equips and empowers our congregations to cross the invisible divides that they might otherwise have no idea about.

As accessible as possible

It is also really important to state that we should not just be thinking about how church meetings are received by people from a working-class background, but by any minority (or even majority) in the community around us. We don't need to bend or shape everything around minorities – indeed, compromise, understanding and acceptance are needed on *all* sides – but it is important to wrestle with some difficult questions so that we can make church as accessible as possible to as many as possible. As the apostle Paul wrote:

> For though I am free from all, I have made myself a servant to all, that I might win more of them . . . I have become all things to all people, that by all means I might save some. I do it all for the sake of the gospel, that I may share with them in its blessings.
>
> (1 Cor. 9.19, 22–23 ESV UK)

Take serving teams in church life, for example. Most of us place a high value on reliability. We want to see Christians who get stuck in – whether it's on the coffee team, setting out the chairs, helping with children's groups or whatever. Our expectation is that people will commit to what they sign up for, turn up faithfully when they're on the rota and spend a significant while in that same serving role. So when that doesn't happen, we might think people are immature Christians, fickle even. But it might be simply that their reliability and faithfulness is being channelled elsewhere. For example, one of my (Natalie's) friends has a reputation as someone who frequently misses church and cancels commitments at the last minute. She comes across as flaky, but in talking through with her what happens on these occasions, it quickly became apparent that she is not uncommitted. She is just more committed elsewhere. So when a relative in her large, extended family is having a crisis, or someone in her immediate neighbourhood needs help, she drops everything to be there for them, to support them in whatever they need. Many around her outside the church consider this to be laudable – family members and neighbours would see her as one of the most reliable people they know. But within the church, this can sometimes be seen as the exact opposite.

The question is not about which approach is better – reliability when we commit to something is really important, and so is flexibility when someone is in trouble and needs our immediate attention. So we are not saying that everyone should be let off the hook, nor that there shouldn't be a challenge when people often renege on their commitments. The point is simply that when we seek to understand what is going on behind the behaviour, we often find that it's not as cut and dried as we might have previously thought.

What we need to consider, then, is how we build teams with people from diverse backgrounds who may have varying allegiances that can influence their commitment level to our particular team, group or meeting structure. It is a difficult question, but one that is worth asking so that we can help people from all walks of life to integrate fully in church life.

Why we do what we do

This kind of thinking – where leaders and teams ask questions about how each element of church life and our meetings is received – will hopefully help us to bring down invisible divides. Examining how we worship, take our offering, set out the chairs, use screens and welcome visitors, and why we do these things the way we do them, is good practice anyway, but it is especially important if we want to ensure that we are not just catering for the majority who are already comfortable with the way we do things. Of course, there will always be some who don't like the way we do things, and that doesn't mean we should automatically make changes – but the question here isn't whether people *like* the way we do things, but whether we put obstacles in their way that mean they cannot engage in church life and feel part of the church community.

The same is true of prayer meetings, youth groups, midweek small groups and so on. Jesus created a discipleship community comprising different types of people. Among his close followers were a tax collector, a zealot, fishermen, and women. These people would not have usually been in close proximity for a prolonged period of time, but Jesus drew them together and they walked with him and each other for three years. There were disagreements and arguments, but they were ultimately united by Christ. And that is how the church is supposed to look – very different people, with diverse backgrounds, united and committed and submitting to each other, outdoing each other in showing honour, accepting one another, laying down their preferences for one another, because of their unity in Christ.

Self-imposed segregation

This goes far beyond sitting in the same church building on a Sunday morning. Sadly, it can be easy for us to think that our church community is a diverse body of believers with no divides, when in fact even where people sit in our meetings reveals that there is self-imposed segregation in our congregations. I was challenged about this by my church leader when I was co-writing one of my earlier books, *A Church for the Poor*. He read a draft manuscript and highlighted a badly written paragraph that made it sound as if I didn't think my own church was a gospel-centred church. I edited what I had written, and it ended up in the published book as this:

> Some of us are in diverse churches but never mix with those in the congregation who are from different backgrounds. A teenager who recently moved from a London borough to my (Natalie's) church said he noticed immediately that black people sit in one section on Sundays – it was so stark to him that he asked if we had set aside that area specifically! This reflects a challenge to our churches to be places where diversity means integration of different types of people. If people from

a working class background, or who are single, or who are elderly, all sit together and do not have meaningful relationships with people 'not like them', we have stopped short of building New Testament churches.[1]

My church leader pointed out graciously that, as I'm on the leadership team in my church, perhaps I might want to do something about this, if I see it in our own setting. So I did. I moved from my regular seat (radical, I know!) to the other side of our auditorium and sat with a group of maybe two dozen students from African nations who had been hand-picked as the best and brightest, and invited to study near my home town, with a view to securing places in the best universities around the world. I sat among them and got to know several of this fascinating group of people over about six months, until they left for their home countries for the summer.

Some conversations were hard at first. I wasn't sure if they wondered what I was doing when I suddenly started sitting in 'their' rows, but everyone was friendly and happy to chat with me, even if we didn't have a huge amount in common at the time. After chatting, I would make a note on my phone of some of the things those I had spoken to that week had mentioned – exams coming up, not sleeping well, that kind of thing – so that I could pray for them and ask them the following week how they were feeling or how exams had gone.

One of the things that was interesting to me, as I responded to this challenge from my church pastor to take the lead myself in walking across the room and mixing with people 'not like me', was how it was perceived by others. For example, one well-meaning woman in the church came up to me a few weeks in to ask if I had fallen out with my friends. She was concerned for me – she assumed I had moved away from my friends in church, rather than moved towards people I didn't know. She wanted to check I was OK and, presumably, to encourage me to restore my relationships if they were broken.

Part of why I found this assumption so fascinating is because, before moving, I always sat with other members of the leadership team of the church (because they're my friends, not because they're leaders), so it would have been especially bad if I had moved to the other side of the auditorium for several weeks because of a falling-out!

It wasn't easy to sit with strangers at first, but I really appreciated the provocation from my pastor to do something about the – in this case visible – divide in our church community, because if we truly want to be the church God has called us to be, then it requires us to get to know people we may initially have very little in common with, except Jesus: not just sitting in the same building, singing the same songs and listening to the same sermons, but actually getting to know each other so that we really can love each other deeply – so that we really can honour, prefer, submit and care for each other. This has to have a meaningful outworking in order for it to be genuine love that shows the world around us that we are Jesus' disciples (see John 13.35).

In a summer 2021 sermon, US church leader Matt Chandler put it like this:

> What binds us, what you and I have most in common is not our upbringing, not where we land on specific social issues. What holds us together is that I was lost and now I'm found, just like you . . . We get to show off the glory of Jesus in how we agree on that, and how we just might disagree on a lot of other stuff, but I still love you and care for you, and you still love and care for me.[2]

'Divide-defying love'

Returning to the subject of our church meetings, even how we deliver our notices and what they're about can have the potential to create barriers, or an 'us and them' culture. But this can be (and often is) more about *who* we involve in the public roles in our meetings than what we say. We'll look at this more in the next chapter exploring the vital role of diversity in leadership or public-facing roles.

When Will Thorburn of London City Mission (LCM) became a Christian, he had no real experience of church life. According to the LCM website, his missionary work today is based at a church 'where they put effort into welcoming people from all walks of life and acknowledge that people are different and have different needs'.[3] This means that they are open to people speaking up during Sunday meetings, something that would be anathema in many evangelical churches! He says:

> If people don't understand, or if they disagree, they will sometimes ask a question in the middle of a service, and that's ok. They are not treated disrespectfully, and the response is not dismissive . . . God doesn't say that only certain people can come to me.[4]

This is a view echoed by LCM Chief Executive Graham Miller, who writes:

> Our Bibles call us to a divide-defying love, where older ladies care for the younger ladies, where the healthy care for the sick, and where we give until we hurt to help the church in need. Yet, too often we become narrow clubs for 'people just like us'.[5]

Changing the way we do meetings, especially if we have conducted them in a certain way for a long time, can be one of the hardest things to do when addressing the issues in this book. It takes effort to examine our traditions and habits, to wrestle with them, to engage minorities among us in honest conversations about them. It takes even more effort to listen and act on what we discover. Plus, of course, any changes we make might leave long-time members of the church disgruntled. We may even lose people. But, as we have already said, the goal is not to hold meetings that everyone likes, but to create meetings that put forward as few barriers as possible to the minorities we would like to see among us, and part of us.

We read in the book of Acts that within the early church there were divisions and dissensions, but we also see diverse communities where Jews and Gentiles, slaves and free, rich and poor, men and women, old and young came together to worship Jesus, compromising their preferences to honour one another and so as to not cause others to stumble in their faith. Surely tweaking the length of our preaching or making our youth camps more affordable is worth it if we find that a wider group of people can access church life as a result. These things may take effort initially, and explanation repeatedly to the majority who are familiar with them, but in the long run they will help us to break down invisible divides and to integrate people from a much broader spectrum of backgrounds into our church communities.

Difficult situations

The danger, if we don't, is that people will feel alienated and excluded. I (Paul) know a mature Christian couple who attended what they described as 'a very middle-class church in a posh town just outside [their] city'. They had grown increasingly frustrated with what they saw as the church's narrow understanding of community. They felt that they didn't fit in, but they compromised culturally because they wanted to be accepted. They even trained themselves to switch into what they called 'church mode': they learnt to conform to certain ways of doing things, even though it wasn't comfortable for either them or their teenage sons. Their sons particularly struggled to find their place in that church community. They became completely disengaged from church life, primarily because they felt they had no connection to the dominant culture. They didn't like the music style and they found the sermons too long and boring. They also thought the 'politeness' of it all was just hypocritical. Perhaps most importantly, they struggled with the fact that they didn't feel they could bring their friends, who didn't know Jesus, along to church on a Sunday morning. Sadly, a conversation with the pastor about all of this managed to cause offence. He wasn't prepared to change the church's style for 'a few people who were different'. Their question was, 'How do we find our place in a church where we can't be authentic?'

These are difficult situations for both church leaders and members to navigate. If leaders were to change something every time a church member expressed dissatisfaction with it, they would probably be changing things every week. But at the same time, if there are clear barriers to how certain people or groups of people engage – people who are wanting to be part of the church community and wanting to invite their non-Christian friends – then surely leaders should listen to those voices sympathetically and explore what adjustments can be made.

Sadly, the situation of the family mentioned above is not a unique one. I (Natalie) have seen friends leave church for various reasons – some to do with them, but some that could have been avoided. For example, one woman left because her struggling eyesight meant she couldn't read the words to new songs. The church could have easily found a way to help in this situation, and indeed might want to think about solutions for people who cannot read for various reasons. Another friend stopped going to church when someone very dear to her died. She said that church was the last place she felt she could go in her grief. That saddened me, because I know that for me it would be the first place I would turn to, so it was a surprise to me that she felt so strongly in the opposite direction.

If we are involved in church leadership or membership, we must learn to appreciate how alien church culture is to many people. And as we do that, we must work hard to preserve the dignity and respect of all who visit or join us. That will probably mean changing the way we do certain things; it will certainly mean a change of attitude and priorities. It will also mean looking for potential leaders in different places, as we'll see in the next chapter.

True diversity will be costly for everyone, but probably most of all for the majority. If we are going to look out for the interests of others and build them into community, that may mean our preaching is less academically stimulating than some would like. It may mean we have to review the style and content of the songs we sing. It could mean that people heckle during a sermon or go outside halfway through for a smoke. It could mean socializing in a very different way from what we are used to.

When it comes to our church community and our church meetings, we are called to be humble and to think of others more than ourselves. It's difficult, but it's the radical discipleship Jesus has called us to.

13

Leadership

If we truly want to change church culture and reach the neglected communities in the UK, one of the things we urgently need to change is how we define what makes a good church leader. We alluded to this briefly in Part 1. There seems to be a lack of leaders who are willing and able to reach out into working-class communities. And there is undoubtedly a lack of leaders who identify as working class.

In the Bible, we see that ordinary people are used by God in extraordinary ways. Social status, education, wealth, qualifications – none of these things are prerequisites for becoming a leader. In fact, God seems to often pick the most unlikely people to lead: 'When they saw the courage of Peter and John and realised that they were unschooled, ordinary men, they were astonished and they took note that these men had been with Jesus' (Acts 4.13).

We stated early on that, inevitably, our churches reflect their leaders. So if church leaders are typically middle class and well educated, then this will be seen across our congregations too. These leaders send potential new leaders

> to colleges run by middle class educated people like them. They, likewise, churn out middle class educated people like them and set requirements that are often only met by middle class educated people like them. Working class people then enter the church and quickly learn this place is not for people like me, leadership is not for people like me and theological training is not for people like me.[1]

If we want to see diverse churches reflecting people from across our communities and bridging invisible divides, we need a radical shift in our thinking, otherwise we will continue to deny leadership roles to the unschooled and ordinary; people who have been shaped by grace and grit rather than traditional scholarship. If we dismiss people as leadership candidates simply because of their background or lack of formal education, we will be excluding some mighty men and women of God. Peter the fisherman probably wouldn't be considered for leadership in most of our churches. If we don't shift our sights when it comes to church leadership then we will inevitably miss some powerful and godly leaders. People like Tommy Medhurst.

Tommy Medhurst

Thomas William Medhurst grew up on the mean streets of Bermondsey, south London, in the mid-nineteenth century. His schooling was rudimentary at best, but formal education wasn't really relevant to his work as a rope-maker's apprentice. Medhurst's neighbours would have known his trade without having to ask him: rope-makers always carried with them the distinctive smell of the tar that they used to waterproof the heavy hemp ropes they made.

Medhurst's lack of education didn't stop him writing to Charles Spurgeon after hearing him preach, anxiously asking, 'How am I to find Jesus? How am I to know that He died for me?'[2]

In Spurgeon's written response, he concluded by saying, 'There is the cross, and a bleeding God-man upon it; look to Him and be saved!'

Medhurst did just that! He 'looked to Christ' and was soundly saved. Almost immediately he began preaching on the streets surrounding the New Street Chapel in Southwark. He was brimming with gospel passion, but some of the church members who heard him preach did not approve. They were outraged at what they called his 'want of education' and that his standard of spoken English left something to be desired. They complained to Mr Spurgeon himself. 'Medhurst should be stopped!' they raged.

When Spurgeon met with the young preacher to discuss their complaints against him, Medhurst's response was definite and sharp: 'I must preach . . . and I *shall* preach unless you cut off my 'ead!'

Spurgeon was suitably impressed, and it was agreed that decapitation wasn't necessary!

Soon, people were being converted and joining the church through that young man's street preaching. Spurgeon took notice and told Medhurst he believed God was calling him to be a preacher and a pastor. The logical next step would be for Medhurst to go to Bible college. However, just like many people today, Medhurst was not seen as suitable ministry material. And there were additional problems. Colleges were expensive, and they assumed that their students would already have achieved a good standard of formal education. On both counts the rough young street preacher would struggle. Spurgeon, however, had faith in him. He would train him himself.

Tommy Medhurst didn't stay preaching on the streets of Southwark. His ministry matured and he went on to pastor churches in London, Coleraine in Ireland, Glasgow and Portsmouth. During his ministry, the apprentice rope-maker from Bermondsey, whose standard of spoken English had so shocked the members of his first church, had personally baptized almost 1,000 converts.

Tommy Medhurst's story should challenge us today.

How gratifying would it be today to see more and more men and women raised up from some of this nation's neglected communities? From the towns and estates from which Christians seem to have fled and then forgotten? From the communities that are still suffering because the traditional industries around which they grew and flourished have all but vanished? These communities are today's equivalent of those vicious Victorian slums whose conditions shocked so many into action. Who will go to them today with that eternal message of hope and good news that Tommy Medhurst preached so passionately?

Raising up working-class leaders

When thinking about the worrying lack of working-class leaders in the church, I (Paul) began to seek out the few leaders I knew from working-class backgrounds, to hear first-hand how they got into ministry. What were their struggles and experiences and how did they respond?

Tom's story

I'd left school at 16 and was working on building sites when I became a Christian.

Quite quickly I realized there was a measure of leadership anointing on me; certainly enough gifting there for some people to recognize it, but I don't think I would have been given the opportunity to lead in a meaningful way apart from the fact that others were removed from leadership roles through either life circumstances or sin. I ended up being the last resort. I was part of a small church plant, and quite soon after it started six middle-class couples moved on for a host of reasons. These people held most of the various leadership roles. The guy who was leading was looking round for someone to pick up some leadership responsibility, and I was pretty much the only one left who knew which way up the Bible was!

After that, a small team of people gave up a year of their time to serve the church plant in outreach. When the fella leading the team suddenly left, I ended up becoming team leader, again by default. We experienced a measure of evangelistic success, which was a surprise to some because I wasn't on their radar for leadership.

Then a caretaker leader was appointed. That was great for me because he was a 'thinking outside the box' kinda guy. And he gave me and a couple of other fellas the opportunity to pick up leadership responsibility that a more conventional middle-class leader probably wouldn't have. That was my first real opportunity in church leadership.

Then the new permanent pastor came along and inherited me as one of his leaders. He begrudgingly had to admit that a significant number of the church were there directly because of my and my wife's work in the community and felt he had to tolerate us. We were very different from him.

When he eventually gave me the opportunity to preach, his comments afterwards were along the lines of, 'That was surprisingly good but next time you preach I want you to have a shave, I want you to wear a shirt and I want you to cut your hair.'

There were a few other things he tried to direct me in that were definitely shaped by his middle-class culture rather than biblical principles. I was willing to have a shave, I was willing to wear a shirt with a collar, but I wasn't going to cut my hair! He wanted me to be something I'm not. He was wanting me to be a carbon copy of himself. I had to say to him, 'I do not want to be like you!' That was hard for him to hear, but that was it.

The truth is, I learnt a lot from that man, but it was more the stuff I caught from him than the stuff where he sat me down to teach me formally.

As a roofer, a working-class guy, I value diversity. When I first went to church, I very much felt part of a minority, but you just get on with it. I suppose that's why I appreciate the breadth of class diversity much more, especially coming into church leadership. Not being arrogant but I felt I had stuff to offer, but it was kind of overlooked because I didn't fit into a certain mould. But now I'm in a position of leadership I'm really passionate about diversity: social diversity, racial diversity – all kinds of diversity! I recognize that my contributions could have been overlooked and missed so I'm aware that people who come into the church who are not like me may well have stuff to offer that I'm going to miss if I'm not careful. They reckon that the best roses are surrounded by the most manure! I think my leadership is stronger because of those early experiences and I'm grateful for the opportunities – or more accurately the lack of opportunities – that I had, because it made them all the more precious to me when I came into church leadership.

The thing that frustrates me is when middle-class values get mixed up with biblical values and therefore people are overlooked. Also, there's a kind of presumption that everyone has access to a computer and everyone knows how to use one. When I was paid on the building site, I was paid a daily rate at the end of the week, not a salary every month. That was something I had to get my head around. Also, because I was a builder, I had never worked in an office before, and I'd never worked with women before, so they were also things that I had to get my head round.

There's a 'one foot in front of the other', earthy walk with God that can sometimes be missed with the spiritual stuff. The stuff I learnt from 25 years of working on the building site you can't learn at Bible college, especially in terms of people's characters – reading people. I don't know if this is true or not, but I think that because of some of the 'orrible people I met on the building, I'm probably more protective of people in the church – certainly the girls, but generally, I think, there's some people who are quite naïve out there. Whether that says more about me negatively than anything else, I'll just put that out there.

Another thing, I have lost people in our church – definitely, because I've spoken straight to them, quite bluntly, and really meant it lovingly. But sometimes it comes out wrong or not couched properly.

And the last thing is that, actually, I don't see a working-class voice in any of the apostolic circles, certainly in the family of churches I'm part of in the main teams – they're all high-flying business types. Some of the strategic 'let's go and take the world' meetings, as far as I know, don't have any working-class voices in them.

Glenn's story

I was sovereignly saved out of a chaotic lifestyle of drink and drugs, crime and self-indulgence. This was through a vision rather than through a church, so I walked with Jesus for two years on my own before really encountering other born-again believers.

During my school years, it's safe to say, I wasn't academically focused! I was actually asked by my teachers to leave school on my sixteenth birthday, before my exams were due to be taken. We all agreed that, for me, school was pointless.

I could never keep a job after I left school. Working 9 to 5 conflicted with my lifestyle. Drink, drugs and whatever exciting experience might come along was much more appealing than a career.

So when Jesus saved me, my lifestyle changed completely. I got clean and sober and ready to engage with the reality of life. But the only employment I could find was as a labourer at a sewage plant. I suppose you could say I started at the bottom!

By obeying God and seeking his will for me, I found myself to be surprisingly employable. At one stage several years later, I ended up with a lucrative job managing the advertising and marketing department of a prestigious magazine.

In some of those secular work scenarios, I often found myself included in conversations about what school or university I'd attended. I developed strategies to avoid giving straight answers. Fortunately, I was never asked outright about my academic achievements, which were of course non-existent! This was probably because of my ability to blag my way through life and into jobs!

Even though I was now employable, I could never shake off a deep sense of God calling me to church leadership, mainly to preach and teach. I have often been disturbed by the church having the same values as the world when discussing leadership potential – e.g., what schools and university they attended, highlighting secular workplace skills. I would rather ask, 'Are they being led by the Holy Spirit? Does this show in their lifestyle? What faith stories do they have?' Not, 'He has a really good job in banking; he would be a real asset to the church.' Or, 'She went to Oxford; she will have so much to offer.'

Although I felt accepted by most people in the church, I quickly became aware that I'd become some sort of grace trophy. Because of my dramatic conversion, I would often be asked to tell my salvation story. It was also made clear to me by the leaders of the church that I wouldn't have the capacity to lead a church because I didn't have the education, administrative skills, financial security or professional experience. I realized, even after years of spiritual growth, they still thought of me as the 'testimony man'.

In my early days I was often the guest speaker, telling my salvation story at various churches. I can remember being avoided by many members as I didn't look like the average middle-class churchgoer.

One memory I have of when I was church planting was being told by another Christian, who had recently joined the plant, that having a dramatic testimony was great, but it was maturity that counted. He had no idea how long I'd been a Christian or what leadership experience I had. He didn't know what I had left behind to join the new church plant, so I can only suppose I must have looked immature, maybe because of my tattoos or accent.

Even today, having been in church leadership for more than 30 years, I often get mistaken for the caretaker, not the pastor. Over the years, when asked what I do for a job, I have come to realize that I must also look like a plasterer! Even recently, the nurse who was administering my second Covid jab asked what job I did. I replied, 'Pastor,' and she responded, 'Oh, we could have done with you a few weeks ago – all the walls and ceiling here needed plastering.' I suppose 'pastor' sounds like 'plasterer'!

I am still disturbed by what some churches look for in their leaders. I've met leaders who know about the goodness of the gospel but hardly seem to know Jesus personally. I am currently the pastor of an Evangelical Free Church in a very affluent part of the country, with many members who are high-flyers and captains of industry. The emphasis of my teaching is often to point people to a faith-driven walk with Jesus.

When it comes to potential preachers and pastors, let us emulate Spurgeon's faith and vision for Tommy Medhurst. Let us not discount people because of their lack of formal education, their accent or their limited vocabulary. If we did, we would have to put aside people like Tommy Medhurst, and my friends Glenn and Tom. In fact, Natalie and I would also be discounted. If we cannot see the value of leaders from working-class cultures, we might question God as to why he made his Son a carpenter rather than a college lecturer!

If we want to raise up leaders from working-class backgrounds, we need to do things very differently. Currently, we tend to conflate background and academic ability with qualification for ministry. When identifying leaders, formal academic qualifications are often a basic requirement. Consequently, the vast majority of church leaders I know are middle-class university graduates. That's not necessarily wrong, but we need to realize that there are huge blind spots and cultural shortcomings built into that particular life experience. And in both Glenn's and Tom's stories, we see that they were on the receiving end of class bias and prejudice.

As one pastor in Greater Manchester puts it:

It is possible to be a wonderful communicator to working class people and yet be rubbish at expressing yourself in academic writing. It is possible to be able to teach without being able to corral your theological knowledge in an exam setting. There is a simple test here: Would most of Jesus' disciples make it through most British theological colleges today? If not, it rather suggests we are placing academic requirements on the ministry that Jesus didn't demand from his apostles and thus neither from elders and pastors.[3]

Uneducated fishermen

When Jesus chose his 'leadership team', he intentionally selected people who would have looked unqualified to those around them – he chose uneducated fishermen, people who would not be considered for leadership in many churches today. And it's self-perpetuating: most church leaders will instinctively look for people like themselves to put forward for leadership training, because that's the type of leadership they are familiar with.

The biblical qualifications for church leadership are primarily related to character, not based on academic achievement. Let's put godly character at the top of the list. We need to challenge long-held beliefs and be very clear that people who are working class are qualified for church ministry as much as anyone else. As a method of training future leaders, I would suggest the example of the apprentice would be more appropriate than that of the university student. And please understand that I am not saying that academic achievement isn't important in a Christian context. It can be, but we must not exclude people because of a lack of qualifications. And even if potential working-class leaders are willing to jump through the hoops of formal qualifications, they can still face prejudice and opposition, as we saw from Tom's and Glenn's experiences.

This nation needs an army of church leaders who haven't been to university to join all those who have. We need those who have struggled with aspects of life that the middle class have not. We need a diversity of leaders if we are to reach a diverse nation. The ones best equipped to reach working-class communities are the working class themselves, or those who have done the hard work of humbling themselves to see things from the perspective of those not like themselves.

We are not saying that middle-class leaders cannot or should not lead in a working-class context. To say that would exclude those well-educated, wealthy leaders who were loved and revered by the working-class communities they devoted themselves to. People like F. B. Meyer.

Middle-class Meyer

Frederick Brotherton Meyer had a happy and secure childhood, enjoying, among other things, games of cricket and playing freely on Clapham Common. He was born into 'an affluent and conventional Victorian family'[4] – his father's occupation was listed as 'Gentleman', having made his money as a successful merchant (although later, he was to lose much of his wealth on the stock exchange).

Meyer was loved by the working-class communities he ministered to, probably because they knew he loved them. He cared about them; he understood their needs. There was the time after hosting a hearty meal for local men when

> Meyer pointed out that working men unlike usual church goers, did not care much for cakes – trays of tobacco were handed around. Meyer didn't like smoking but, he wrote, 'It has always been a habit of mine in these things to let God's Spirit dictate what a man shall do and shall not do. We have no right to add to the Ten Commandments in the earlier stages of the Christian Life.' At this occasion, Meyer was full of banter and humour. The men took to him.[5]

He was held in high regard even by the rough working men of late Victorian Lambeth. There's a well-known story of a time Meyer was speaking at a temperance meeting and was being heckled loudly by one in the audience:

> A burly workman turned round and said quietly but firmly, 'Shut up, you fool. That's Meyer, as good a man as ever stepped in shoe leather. You don't know that man, or you'd soon dry up.' He did dry up.[6]

Whether we are unschooled fishermen or bricklayers or the children of gentlemen, let us have humility to reach out to those around us, motivated by God's love, a robust, biblical love that challenges us to go to the often despised and to the feared and to shine his light into the working-class communities up and down this nation.

Conclusion

The Bible paints a glorious picture of what the church will look like when Jesus returns. At the end of the age, the fullness of what the apostle Paul wrote to the Galatians – that 'there is neither Jew nor Greek, there is neither slave nor free, there is no male or female, for you are all one in Christ Jesus' (Gal. 3.28 ESV UK) – will become the reality. The 'dividing wall of hostility' (Eph. 2.14) that Jesus has broken down will be completely removed, and there will be total unity between all disciples.

What John saw in his revelation on Patmos island was this:

> a great multitude that no one could number, from every nation, from all tribes and peoples and languages, standing before the throne and before the Lamb, clothed in white robes, with palm branches in their hands, and crying out with a loud voice, 'Salvation belongs to our God who sits on the throne, and to the Lamb!'
> (Rev. 7.9–10 ESV UK)

This is what the church will look like in the end: a beautifully diverse multitude – thousands upon thousands upon thousands of people with vastly differing backgrounds and lives – worshipping together in complete unity in Christ. There will be no divisions, no barriers, nothing that will exclude or alienate or ostracize. Every single person will belong there, and know they belong there, not because they meet certain criteria, but because God chose them to be part of his family.

When we look at the church across the world today, or perhaps even in our own city or community, it can feel as though we are very far from God's plan. We are fallible humans who easily lapse into negative ways of thinking about others. As Paul and I have written this book, I have been aware of specific prejudices and judgemental attitudes in my own heart. When that happens, I repent and ask God to increasingly align my heart with his, my thoughts with his. From that place of repentance, I then have to work hard to spot such attitudes when they arise and deal with them quickly. I also have a handful of close friends whom I have invited to challenge me on anything like this that they see in me. After repenting, I attempt to question my thinking, analyse why I think the way I do and then try to tackle it head on. This is often a painful process. It's humbling. But it's necessary if I'm to obey Jesus, who said, 'By this everyone will know that you are my disciples, if you love one another' (John 13.35).

Putting up walls

There are all kinds of walls we can put up, both consciously and subconsciously. Most are designed to protect us – to keep ourselves, our loved ones, our way of life safe from outside harm – rather than to keep others out. Yet that is what they do. When this happens in church life, it creates a culture that is usually formed around the dominant group of people within that setting. It's understandable that this happens, but it still needs to be challenged. Our individual lives and our church communities are enriched by diversity. That's true of all kinds of diversity, but we have chosen to focus on the often-neglected subject of class differences.

Class differences run deep, as we have seen. They affect all areas of our lives. Some of our faith battles are different – the way we interpret what it means to live a life of faith might vary enormously. Our starting premise for how we view church can be wildly different, because of how we think about community, what it means to us and what other allegiances we bring to the table. How we think about and handle our money is often not the same – and therefore what it means to us to be generous can differ too. Whether we fear or welcome authority will depend on our previous experiences of it. The way we speak – not just our accents, but the language we use, the way we banter and how blunt we are – is influenced by our background. What motivates us is not the same. Our aspirations are, generally speaking, quite different.

Despite the challenges these differences present, we are still called to be part of God's church family together. God's vision for the church is not to have one church over here that caters to the working classes and another over here for the middle classes, and so on and so on for as many groups of people as exist within each community. No. His vision is for us to be alongside each other within local church communities, honouring one another, loving and learning from one another, overcoming the things that would divide us, for his glory and for the good of the world around us. When people outside our churches look in on us, they should notice how we love each other despite our differences.

It's not that the differences should be erased. We aren't called to conform to the image of those around us. Our differences should be visible, yet our love for each other should be so unmistakable that it causes people around us to ask questions. Ultimately, it should point them to Jesus, the one who has brought us all together into the same family.

The process of becoming churches like that will be tough, but it is vital. The starting point is identifying the invisible divides – those things that previously we had not seen or understood. We cannot change what we can't see. Raising awareness in our own minds, and then among our church families, is crucial if we are to start to become all that God intended us to be – places where the groups and subcultures that are found in the communities around us are also found to be thriving in our church communities. An awareness of the divisions between us – the miscommunications, the misunderstandings and the misconceptions – will empower us to change. Knowing the issues that have the potential to exclude or offend is the first step towards being able to address them.

But awareness is only the beginning. We need to harness that knowledge and use it to change our own attitudes, as well as the activities and habits of our churches. If you are a church leader, it is so important to create spaces for open conversations about the things that can cause hostility and division among us. It requires huge doses of humility on all sides: every one of us needs to lay down our preferences, our perceived rights, our traditions and ways of doing things, so that others are welcomed and integrated and can become true members of the church family.

For all followers of Jesus, our identity is first and foremost that we are children of God. Every other aspect of our identity comes second to this. We may find and formulate our identity in many different ways, but our primary identity is based on our relationship with Jesus, not with any other group, nor any other place, nor any other allegiance in our lives. This is what unites us. We are all Jesus-followers first, and everything else comes after that.

There are many invisible divides between the different classes, but none is insurmountable within the church. Opening our eyes to see them, then creating a healthy culture of communication and openness about them will lead us in the right direction. Jesus has called his church to break down every barrier and to find unity in him. One day we will see the fulfilment of that. But for now, let's play our part in crossing invisible divides and seeing people from all classes and walks of life come to know him, worship him and serve him together, for his glory.

About Jubilee+

Jubilee+ is a UK charity that equips churches of all denominations to be increasingly effective in bringing mercy and justice to those around them. Our vision is to see local churches actively playing their part in changing the lives of those trapped in poverty in their communities.

The changes we aim to bring about are:

Changed churches – churches where changing the lives of people in poverty in their community is a fundamental part of their focus, vision and values.

Changed lives – where people are empowered to live a life free from all forms of poverty.

Changed communities – churches known in their communities as places of help and hope for those in poverty.

To find out more about Jubilee+ and how we do this, or to partner with us, find us at: <jubilee-plus.org> or on social media @jubileeplus.

Notes

Introduction

1 'Social Class: Highlights', British Social Attitudes 33, <www.bsa.
natcen.ac.uk/latest-report/british-social-attitudes-33/social-class.
aspx>

2 'Social Class', British Social Attitudes 33.

3 'Social Class', British Social Attitudes 33.

4 'Social Class', British Social Attitudes 33, p. 15.

5 'Coronavirus (COVID-19) latest insights', Office for National
Statistics, 8 October 2021, <www.ons.gov.uk/peoplepopulation
andcommunity/healthandsocialcare/conditionsanddiseases/
articles/coronaviruscovid19roundup/2020-03-26#deathsbyarea>;
Dave Burke, 'Coronavirus: People in deprived areas twice as likely
to die as North-South gap opens', *Mirror*, 1 May 2020, <www.
mirror.co.uk/news/uk-news/coronavirus-people-deprived-areas-
twice-21952284>; 'Coronavirus: Higher death rate in poorer areas,
ONS figures suggest', BBC News, 1 May 2020, <www.bbc.co.uk/
news/uk-52506979>.

6 Barna Group, 'Perceptions of Jesus, Christians & Evangelism
in England', Talking Jesus, 2015, <talkingjesus.org/
wp-content/uploads/2018/04/Perceptions-of-Jesus-Christians-
and-Evangelism-Executive-Summary.pdf>, referenced in Martin
Charlesworth and Natalie Williams, *A Church for the Poor:
Transforming the Church to Reach the Poor in Britain Today*
(Eastbourne: David C Cook, 2017), p. 69.

7 <www.jubilee-plus.org>.

8 Roger Lloyd, *The Church and the Artisan Today* (London:
Longmans Green and Co., 1952), p. 54.

9 David Martyn Lloyd-Jones, 'The French Revolution and After',

The Christian and the State in Revolutionary Times (Westminster Conference, 1975), p. 110.

10 Tim Chester, *Unreached: Growing Churches in Working-class and Deprived Areas* (Nottingham: Inter-Varsity Press, 2012), p. 13.

11 Gillian Evans, 'Common ground', *The Guardian*, 4 October 2006, <www.theguardian.com/society/2006/oct/04/communities. guardiansocietysupplement>.

12 Lee Bok, *The Little Book of Chavs: The Branded Guide to Britain's New Elite* (e-book, Bath: Crombie Jardine, 2013. Original paperback 2004; updated 2006).

1 The missing class

1 Craig Groeschel Leadership Podcast, episode 6: 'Creating a Value-Driven Culture, part 2', <www.life.church/leadershippodcast/ creating-a-value-driven-culture-part-2/>.

2 Lynne Cullens, 'A middle-class culture dominates the Church', *Church Times*, 1 March 2019, <https://www. churchtimes.co.uk/articles/2019/1-march/comment/ opinion/a-middle-class-culture-dominates-the-church>.

3 'Bishop says that the Church has forgotten the poor', Anglican Communion News Service, 4 August 2017, <www.anglicannews. org/news/2017/08/bishop-says-that-the-church-has-forgotten-the-poor.aspx>.

4 Philip North, '"Hope for the Poor": A Talk to the New Wine "United" Conference 2017', <www.blackburn.anglican.org/storage/ general-files/shares/Resources/Talks%20articles%20and%20 sermons/Hope_for_the_Poor_-__P_article__Word_document_. pdf>, p. 6.

5 Philip North, '"Hope for the Poor"', pp. 5–6.

6 Gary Jenkins, 'Where are the working class?', guest blogger on Ian Paul's Psephizo, 1 December 2020, <www.psephizo.com/ life-ministry/where-are-the-working-class/>.

7 Gary Jenkins, 'Where are the working class?'

8 Paul Kerley, 'What is your 21st Century social class?', BBC News, 7 December 2015, <www.bbc.co.uk/news/magazine-34766169>.

2 The call to discipleship

1 Gary Jenkins, 'Where are the working class?', guest blogger on Ian Paul's Psephizo, 1 December 2020, <www.psephizo.com/life-ministry/where-are-the-working-class/>.

2 In fact, the phrase is used 100 times in the New Testament. We are instructed, for example, to love one another (John 13.34), build up one another (Rom. 14.19), be humble towards one another (1 Pet. 5.5), spur on one another to love and good deeds (Heb. 10:24), speak truth to one another (Eph. 4.15), accept one another (Rom. 15.7).

3 Martin Charlesworth and Natalie Williams, 'A Life of Simplicity', chapter 3 in *A Call to Act: Building a Poverty-Busting Lifestyle* (Colorado Springs: David C Cook, 2020), pp. 63–84.

3 Faith

1 Martin Charlesworth and Natalie Williams, *A Call to Act* (Colorado Springs: David C Cook, 2020), pp. 33–35.

2 'Which jobs are most likely to have seen a drop in pay during the pandemic?', Office of National Statistics, 5 March 2021, <www.ons.gov.uk/visualisations/dvc1227/index.html>.

4 Communication

1 See Twitter thread at <twitter.com/Digbylj/status/1421164856527437825>, posted on 30 July 2021. For an example of national news coverage of this, see Miranda Bryant, 'BBC's Alex Scott "proud" of working class accent after peer's elocution jibe', *The Guardian*, 31 July 2021, <www.theguardian.com/inequality/2021/jul/31/bbc-alex-scott-proud-working-class-accent-digby-jones-elocution>.

2 See Twitter thread at <twitter.com/AlexScott/status/142125734741

9213831>, posted on 31 July 2021. For an example of national news coverage of this, see Miranda Bryant, 'BBC's Alex Scott "proud" of working class accent after peer's elocution jibe'.

3 Cited in 'Social class: denied and despised', *The Guardian*, 3 April 2013, <https://www.theguardian.com/commentisfree/2013/apr/03/social-class-denied-and-despised>.

4 'Accent bias exists but people can resist the urge to discriminate', Queen Mary University of London, 11 November 2019, <www.qmul.ac.uk/media/news/2019/hss/accent-bias-exists-but-people-can-resist-the-urge-to-discriminate.html>.

5 Derek Rigby, 'Holy disordered', *The Guardian*, 14 July 2008, <https://www.theguardian.com/commentisfree/2008/jul/14/religion>.

6 Gillian Evans, *Educational Failure and Working Class White Children in Britain* (Basingstoke: Palgrave MacMillan, 2006, 2007), pp. 27–28.

5 Hospitality

1 Grant R. Osborne, *Matthew: Zondervan Exegetical Commentary on the New Testament* (Grand Rapids: Zondervan, 2010), p. 336.

2 As heard during a conference at Ashburnham Place, East Sussex, England, in January 2017.

6 Money and generosity

1 Alessandro Malito, 'The unexpected link between social status and generosity', MarketWatch, 7 July 2018, <https://www.marketwatch.com/story/the-unexpected-link-between-social-status-and-generosity-2018-07-03>.

2 Danny Baker, *Going to Sea in a Sieve: The Autobiography* (London: Weidenfeld and Nicholson, 2012), pp. 112, 113.

3 'What Did Wesley Practice and Preach About Money', West Ohio Conference, December 2019, <www.westohioumc.org/conference/news/what-did-wesley-practice-and-preach-about-money>.

7 Community

1 David Cannadine, *Class in Britain* (London: Penguin, 2000), p. 183.

2 Bob Holman, *Faith in the Poor: Britain's Poor Reveal What It's Really Like to Be 'Socially Excluded'* (Oxford: Lion Publishing, 1998), p. 11.

3 'East Sussex', City Population, <www.citypopulation.de/en/uk/admin/E10000011__east_sussex/>.

4 'Overview of Southwark's Population JSNA Factsheet', Southwark Council, July 2018, <file:///C:/Users/nicki/Downloads/JSNA%20Factsheet%202018-19%20-%20Demography%2020180725.pdf>, p. 6.

8 Us and them: attitudes to authority

1 'Trust in professions: Long-term trends', Ipsos MORI, 30 November 2017, <https://www.ipsos.com/ipsos-mori/en-uk/trust-professions-long-term-trends>.

2 'Ipsos MORI Veracity Index 2020', Ipsos Mori, 26 November 2020, <https://www.ipsos.com/ipsos-mori/en-uk/ipsos-mori-veracity-index-2020-trust-in-professions>.

3 '20: Millwall FC (1970s) – No-One Likes Us, We Don't Care', *Creative Review* (undated), <www.creativereview.co.uk/no-one-likes-us-we-dont-care/>.

4 Gillian Evans, *Educational Failure and Working Class White Children in Britain* (Basingstoke: Palgrave MacMillan, 2006, 2007), pp. 31–32.

5 The Secret Barrister, *The Secret Barrister, Stories of the Law and How It's Broken* (London: Picador, 2019), pp. 56–57.

6 The Secret Barrister, *The Secret Barrister*, p. 58.

7 Gillan Scott, 'Should Christians strike?', God & Politics in the UK, 1 December 2011, <godandpoliticsuk.org/2011/12/01/should-christians-strike/>.

9 Motivations

1 Cited in 'Hidden rules among classes', Word on the Streets, 17 October 2016, <www.wordonthestreets.net/articles/481670/hidden_rules_among.aspx>.
2 Martin Charlesworth and Natalie Williams, *A Church for the Poor: Transforming the Church to Reach the Poor in Britain Today* (Eastbourne: David C Cook, 2017), p. 126.

10 Aspirations

1 See <www.compassionuk.org/>.
2 Martin Charlesworth and Natalie Williams, *The Myth of the Undeserving Poor: A Christian Response to Poverty in Britain Today* (Tolworth: Grosvenor House Publishing, 2014), p. 73.
3 'The Effects of Poverty', Child Poverty Action Group (undated), <cpag.org.uk/child-poverty/effects-poverty>.
4 Tim Keller, 'In The Image Of God', YouTube, 22 January 2019, <https://www.youtube.com/watch?v=5H_4UJfOigA&ab_channel=LivingWord>.
5 John Piper, 'What Does It Mean to Be Made in God's Image?', Desiring God, 19 August 2013, <www.desiringgod.org/interviews/what-does-it-mean-to-be-made-in-gods-image>.
6 G. K. Chesterton, *The Scandal of Father Brown* (London: Cassell & Company, 1935), page unknown.
7 Tim Keller, 'In The Image Of God'.

12 Meetings

1 Martin Charlesworth and Natalie Williams, *A Church for the Poor: Transforming the Church to Reach the Poor in Britain Today* (Eastbourne: David C Cook, 2017), pp. 124–125.
2 Matt Chandler, 'Do Not Quench Him', Village Church sermons, 2 August 2021.
3 'Stepping into a Whole New World', London City Mission (undated), <https://www.lcm.org.uk/blog/2020/02/27/stepping-into-a-whole-new-world>.

4 'Stepping into a Whole New World'.
5 'Good News for the Poor', London City Mission (undated), <www.lcm.org.uk/blog/2017/08/25/good-news-for-the-poor-pt-1>.

13 Leadership

1 Stephen Kneale, cited in Matthew Evans, 'The problem of a white, middle-class, academically-educated church', Affinity, 25 January 2018, <www.affinity.org.uk/news/news-stories/post/398-the-problem-of-a-white-middle-class-academically-educated-church>. See also Stephen Kneale, 'Are Theological Colleges the Servant of the Church?', Building Jerusalem, 15 January 2018, <www.buildingjerusalem.blog/2018/01/15/are-theological-colleges-the-servant-of-the-church/>.
2 Elements of our retelling of Tommy Medhurst's story are based on chapter 9, 'The Pastors' College', in Peter Morden, *The People's Preacher: C. H. Spurgeon* (Waverley: CWR, 2009).
3 Stephen Kneale, 'Are Theological Colleges the Servant of the Church?'
4 Bob Holman, *F. B. Meyer: If I Had A Hundred Lives . . .* (Fearn, Ross-shire: Christian Focus Publications Ltd, 2007), p. 11.
5 Holman, *F. B. Meyer*, p. 78.
6 Holman, *F. B. Meyer*, p. 83.

Bibliography

Books

Baker, Danny, *Going to Sea in a Sieve: The Autobiography* (London: Weidenfeld and Nicholson, 2012).

Bok, Lee, *The Little Book of Chavs: The Branded Guide to Britain's New Elite* (e-book, Bath: Crombie Jardine, 2013. Original paperback, 2004; updated 2006).

Cannadine, David, *Class in Britain* (London: Penguin, 2000).

Charlesworth, Martin and Natalie Williams, *A Call to Act: Building a Poverty-Busting Lifestyle* (Colorado Springs: David C Cook, 2020).

Charlesworth, Martin and Natalie Williams, *A Church for the Poor: Transforming the Church to Reach the Poor in Britain Today* (Eastbourne: David C Cook, 2017).

Charlesworth, Martin and Natalie Williams, *The Myth of the Undeserving Poor: A Christian Response to Poverty in Britain Today* (Tolworth: Grosvenor House Publishing, 2014).

Chester, Tim, *Unreached: Growing Churches in Working-class and Deprived Areas* (Nottingham: Inter-Varsity Press, 2012).

Evans, Gillian, *Educational Failure and Working Class White Children in Britain* (Basingstoke: Palgrave MacMillan, 2006, 2007).

Holman, Bob, *Faith in the Poor: Britain's Poor Reveal What It's Really Like to Be 'Socially Excluded'* (Oxford: Lion Publishing, 1998).

Holman, Bob, *F. B. Meyer: If I Had A Hundred Lives . . .* (Fearn, Ross-shire, Christian Focus Publications Ltd, 2007).

Lloyd, Roger, *The Church and the Artisan Today* (London: Longmans, Green and Co., 1952).

Lloyd-Jones, David Martyn, 'The French Revolution and After', *The Christian and the State in Revolutionary Times* (The Westminster Conference, 1975).

Morden, Peter, *The People's Preacher: C. H. Spurgeon* (Waverley: CWR, 2009).

Osborne, Grant R., *Matthew: Exegetical Commentary on the New Testament* (Grand Rapids: Zondervan, 2010).

The Secret Barrister, *The Secret Barrister: Stories of the Law and How It's Broken* (London: Picador, 2019).

Articles

'20: Millwall FC (1970s) – No-One Likes Us, We Don't Care', *Creative Review* (undated), <www.creativereview.co.uk/no-one-likes-us-we-dont-care/>.

'Accent bias exists but people can resist the urge to discriminate', Queen Mary University of London, 11 November 2019, <www.qmul.ac.uk/media/news/2019/hss/accent-bias-exists-but-people-can-resist-the-urge-to-discriminate.html>.

Barna Group, 'Perceptions of Jesus, Christians & Evangelism in England', *Talking Jesus* (2015), <talkingjesus.org/wp-content/uploads/2018/04/Perceptions-of-Jesus-Christians-and-Evangelism-Executive-Summary.pdf>.

'Bishop says that the Church has forgotten the poor', Anglican Communion News Service, 4 August 2017, <www.anglican news.org/news/2017/08/bishop-says-that-the-church-has-forgotten-the-poor.aspx>.

Bryant, Miranda, 'BBC's Alex Scott "proud" of working class accent after peer's elocution jibe', *The Guardian*, 31 July 2021, <www.theguardian.com/inequality/2021/jul/31/bbc-alex-scott-proud-working-class-accent-digby-jones-elocution>.

Burke, Dave, 'Coronavirus: People in deprived areas twice as likely to die as North-South gap opens', *Mirror*, 1 May 2020, <www.mirror.co.uk/news/uk-news/coronavirus-people-deprived-areas-twice-21952284>.

Chandler, Matt, 'Do Not Quench Him', Village Church sermons, 2 August 2021.

'Coronavirus (COVID-19) latest insights', Office for National Statistics, <www.ons.gov.uk/peoplepopulationandcommunity/ healthandsocialcare/conditionsanddiseases/articles/ coronaviruscovid19roundup/2020-03-26#deathsbyarea>.

'Coronavirus: Higher death rate in poorer areas, ONS figures suggest', BBC News, 1 May 2020, <www.bbc.co.uk/news/uk-52506979>.

Cullens, Lynne, 'A middle-class culture dominates the Church', *Church Times*, 1 March 2019, <https://www.churchtimes.co.uk/ articles/2019/1-march/comment/opinion/a-middle-class-culture-dominates-the-church>.

'East Sussex', City Population, <www.citypopulation.de/en/uk/ admin/E10000011__east_sussex/>.

'The Effects of Poverty', Child Poverty Action Group (undated), <cpag.org.uk/child-poverty/effects-poverty>.

Evans, Gillian, 'Common ground, *The Guardian*, 4 October 2006 <www.theguardian.com/society/2006/oct/04/communities. guardiansocietysupplement>.

Evans, Matthew, 'The problem of a white, middle-class, academically-educated church', Affinity, 25 January 2018, <www.affinity.org.uk/news/news-stories/post/398-the-problem-of-a-white-middle-class-academically-educated-church>.

'Good News for the Poor', London City Mission (undated), <www. lcm.org.uk/blog/2017/08/25/good-news-for-the-poor-pt-1>.

Groeschel, Craig, Leadership Podcast, episode 6: 'Creating a Value-Driven Culture, part 2', <www.life.church/leadershippodcast/ creating-a-value-driven-culture-part-2/>.

'Hidden rules among classes', Word on the Streets, 17 October 2016, <www.wordonthestreets.net/articles/481670/hidden_ rules_among.aspx>.

'Ipsos MORI Veracity Index 2020', Ipsos Mori, 26 November 2020, <https://www.ipsos.com/ipsos-mori/en-uk/ipsos-mori-veracity-index-2020-trust-in-professions>.

Jenkins, Gary, 'Where are the working class?', guest blogger on Ian Paul's Psephizo, 1 December 2020, <www.psephizo.com/life-ministry/where-are-the-working-class/>.

Kerley, Paul, 'What is your 21st Century social class?', BBC News, 7 December 2015, <www.bbc.co.uk/news/magazine-34766169>.

Kneale, Stephen, 'Are Theological Colleges the Servant of the Church?', Building Jerusalem, 15 January 2018, <www.building jerusalem.blog/2018/01/15/are-theological-colleges-the-servant-of-the-church/>.

Malito, Alessandro, 'The unexpected link between social status and generosity', MarketWatch, 7 July 2018, <https://www.marketwatch.com/story/the-unexpected-link-between-social-status-and-generosity-2018-07-03>.

North, Philip, '"Hope for the Poor": A Talk to the New Wine "United" Conference 2017', <www.blackburn.anglican.org/storage/general-files/shares/Resources/Talks%20articles%20and%20sermons/Hope_for_the_Poor_-__P_article__Word_document_.pdf>.

Overview of Southwark's Population JSNA Factsheet, published by Southwark Council, July 2018, <file:///C:/Users/nicki/Downloads/JSNA%20Factsheet%202018-19%20-%20Demography%2020180725.pdf>.

Piper, John, 'What Does It Mean to Be Made in God's Image?', Desiring God, 19 August 2013, <www.desiringgod.org/interviews/what-does-it-mean-to-be-made-in-gods-image>.

Rigby, Derek, 'Holy disordered', The Guardian, 14 July 2008, <https://www.theguardian.com/commentisfree/2008/jul/14/religion>.

Scott, Gillan, 'Should Christians strike?', God & Politics in the UK, 1 December 2011, <godandpoliticsuk.org/2011/12/01/should-christians-strike/>.

'Social Class: Highlights', British Social Attitudes 33, <www.bsa.natcen.ac.uk/latest-report/british-social-attitudes-33/social-class.aspx>.

'Social Class: Identity, awareness and political attitudes: why are we still working class?' (full report), British Social Attitudes 33, <www.bsa.natcen.ac.uk/media/39094/bsa33_social-class_v5.pdf>.

'Stepping into a Whole New World', London City Mission (undated), <https://www.lcm.org.uk/blog/2020/02/27/stepping-into-a-whole-new-world>.

'Trust in professions: Long-term trends', Ipsos MORI, 30 November 2017, <https://www.ipsos.com/ipsos-mori/en-uk/trust-professions-long-term-trends>.

'What Did Wesley Practice and Preach About Money', West Ohio Conference, December 2019, <www.westohioumc.org/conference/news/what-did-wesley-practice-and-preach-about-money>.

'Which jobs are most likely to have seen a drop in pay during the pandemic?', Office of National Statistics, 5 March 2021, <www.ons.gov.uk/visualisations/dvc1227/index.html>.

Websites

Compassion, <www.compassionuk.org/>.

Jubilee+, <jubilee-plus.org>.

Bibliography